LET'S DO THIS THING CALLED LIFE!

LET'S *DO* THIS THING CALLED LIFE!

A Guide to Abundant Living

DEBORAH ARSENEAU

Hardcover ISBN: 979-8-9902481-1-3
Paperback ISBN: 979-8-9902481-9-9
eBook ISBN: 979-8-9902481-0-6
Audiobook ISBN: 979-8-9902481-4-4

CONTENTS

This book is dedicated to those who've questioned their abilities. May you never question them again.

INTRODUCTION

Thank God we are a work in progress and can change each day.

For years, I wanted to follow my dreams but never took action. I procrastinated, made excuses, and was distracted. I was living in my comfort zone. I wasn't consciously driving my life to the destination that I desired.

We are born co-creators—that's our gift from God—but how much time do we spend creating positive change in our lives? If you are looking for a better life, if you have a dream you want to pursue but haven't, know that you're not alone.

I am three years into my new journey, and I've written a book. So, what changed? What made this time different? The answer is simple: I changed. I am not the same person I used to be.

How did I move my dream out of my imagination and into reality? I gave it attention. Focus gives life to our desires. I also adopted abundant beliefs, lived by faith, raised my standards, applied my higher mental faculties, changed my habits, became disciplined, remained consistent, overcame obstacles, and revealed my authentic self. When you change on the inside, the outside follows.

These steps of self-empowerment created a new me. I don't even recognize the person I used to be: riddled with fear, afraid to step into the unknown, and worried about the opinions of others. Today, I look at life with fresh eyes and a childlike spirit. It's a wonderful feeling to be excited about the future. Now, the question is "What's next?"

I spent the majority of my life studying the great leaders in the personal development industry: Bob Proctor, Neville Goddard, Dr. Wayne Dyer, Og Mandino, Napoleon Hill, Florence Scovel Shinn, Don Miguel Ruiz, Louise Hay, and countless others. However, my greatest transformations were the result of my life lessons. It was by overcoming struggle, suffering, mistakes, challenges, and fear that I became stronger, wiser, and more faithful. It was through those trials that I gained a better understanding of myself.

Life lessons, once learned, bear the gift of awareness, allowing you to see the error of your ways so you can reroute your path to create a better tomorrow. Unknowingly, all along, I was preparing for my life's purpose: to share the knowledge and wisdom that I've gained along the way.

The secret to life is to know yourself. *You* are the greatest subject you will ever study and ever learn. It's through self-awareness, self-reflection, and self-realization that you can reinvent yourself and live your ideal life, knowing that abundance is your birthright.

To claim that birthright, however, you must *believe* you are worthy of a better life—because your beliefs determine your actions. Therefore, your mindset can be your greatest asset or greatest deterrent; it determines whether you limit yourself or aim for the stars. So you must do things you haven't done before. You must remove false beliefs, self-limiting behaviors, and the stealers of time: procrastination, distractions, and excuses. When you build your life on a solid foundation of abundance, apply your mental faculties, and take a leap of faith, you rise because you step into your fullness.

Remember, nobody can be who you are. Your heart is rare, and your soul contains an essence that cannot be recaptured. You are one of a kind. Therefore, your God-given talents and abilities should not lie dormant, as your inspired actions have the power to change your life and the lives of others; your focused efforts can create a lasting legacy.

This life-changing truth led to the intention behind this book: to empower future generations by equipping them with intellectual, emotional, and spiritual richness—the knowledge required to create a dream life. Please join me as we bring these hidden truths to light and reveal how to *Do This Thing Called Life!*

CHAPTER 1

BELIEFS

When I unfolded the piece of paper that had been slipped into my locker, my eyes fixated on the words "undercover narc." *What is this?* It was my first week at a new high school, and I was receiving a threatening note.

Why would they think I was a narc? Because I started midsemester, or because I acted mature for my age? I just wanted to fit in, but what I encountered was the exact opposite. Could it have been my fear-based thoughts and false beliefs that attracted this experience?

Growing up, my family went through some tough times financially. We moved around a lot, and I attended several different schools. Those challenging experiences made me grow up fast, but they also led to a scarcity mindset and a false sense of insecurity. For decades, the outer instability that I experienced at a young age created inner instability.

How do I know this to be true? Because my main focus in life was working to create a stable environment. It wasn't about going on lavish vacations and creating joyful experiences. It was about saving for a rainy day and paying off debt.

We design our lives according to our beliefs, but our beliefs are shaped by outside influences during our formative years. They are made up of our experiences, our environment, what we've been told and accepted to be true, and the observations of those closest to us: parents, guardians, teachers, etc. Your belief system is the program that runs your life and creates your reality.

Psychologists believe most of our beliefs and habits are established by the age of seven.[1] Let's stop and think about this for a minute. We are God's highest form of creation, so why on earth would we go through our adult lives creating future experiences based on the belief system of a second grader? This sounds foolish, right? What if our childhood experiences consisted of bullying, financial issues, parental separation, abandonment, illness in the family, or any other number of hardships? What if the information we downloaded and believed to be true was inaccurate?

If that's not eye-opening enough, think about this: As we move through life facing challenging situations that result in feelings of inadequacy, we continue to reinforce our false beliefs. These false beliefs then form our shadow side, which contains our fears, insecurities, and emotional baggage from the past.

This information was gold to me. I didn't know that fear-based experiences create false beliefs, which create mental and emotional blockages that can keep you from reaching your true potential. I didn't know that to create a more desirable life, false beliefs must be replaced with abundant beliefs. Previously, my

---

1   Carol Fox, "By the Age of 7 Most of Our Beliefs and Habits Are Formed," LinkedIn, March 7, 2019, https://www.linkedin.com/pulse/age-7-most-our-beliefs-habits-formed-carol-fox/.

life was a series of reactions to the program that was playing out in my subconscious mind. I wasn't consciously steering my life in the direction of my choice; my limited thinking and false beliefs led me to experience life through my fear-based emotions.

What I didn't realize as a child is that stability is found within. Stability is being aware of your inner dialogue, believing in yourself, trusting your intuition, knowing your worth, having abundant beliefs, and regulating your thoughts and emotions. It's remaining steadfast despite life's trials and tribulations, knowing that when you are calm within, you are calm without.

According to an article in *New Scientist*, an estimated 95 percent of the brain's activity happens below the level of consciousness, which means only 5 percent is conscious.[2] That's why it's imperative to eliminate false beliefs: we are on autopilot the majority of the time, which means the subconscious mind is in control.

When you harbor false beliefs, they cast a shadow of doubt over you, creating a scarcity mindset and low self-esteem, which leads to insecurities, such as self-defeating thoughts, a lack of self-belief, and feelings of unworthiness, uncertainty, and inadequacy. They can also lead to codependent relationships and living in your comfort zone. False beliefs inhibit your growth because they are created out of fear. They will tell you that you're not good enough, which can keep you from reaching your full potential.

When you don't know your worth, you live by the fake program playing out in your subconscious mind. The subconscious mind is emotional, not logical. It's a memory bank that contains your beliefs, your habits of thinking and acting, and the memories and emotions associated with all of your

---

2   Emma Young, "Lifting the Lid on the Unconscious," *New Scientist*, July 25, 2018, https://www.newscientist.com/article/mg23931880-400-lifting-the-lid-on-the-unconscious/.

experiences; therefore, it projects *who you believe you are, what you believe, and how you feel,* thereby creating your life experiences. It runs as a continuous loop until you break the cycle. With this fact in mind, you must cultivate self-awareness and know your worth so that your identity is one of love, not fear, because fear is holding on to false beliefs, which makes you feel inferior and afraid.

How your mind is programmed determines the trajectory of your life. In order to achieve positive results, you must reprogram your subconscious mind by thinking abundant thoughts and feeling abundant. The subconscious mind follows the conscious mind's lead. So, let's hang a sign in our homes that reads: *I am abundant, and abundance consciousness is the best place to hang out!*

False Beliefs

How do you identify false beliefs? False beliefs are communicated through your critical inner voice. They are self-limiting thoughts that keep you from moving forward and don't support your growth.

ACTION STEP 1: Take out a piece of paper. On the left-hand side, write down the false beliefs that are holding you back, and on the right-hand side, write down the opposite of each belief.
For example:
I am unworthy of my dreams. I am worthy of my dreams!
I am too old. I am the perfect age!
I don't have experience. I am gaining experience!
By writing down your beliefs, you can identify which ones are limiting your progress.

Notice how many times the word "identify" is used throughout this book. When you identify with something, it's because it reflects what you believe, who you are, and what you do.

ACTION STEP 2: Place an "X" over the false beliefs that you wrote down. This action tells the subconscious mind that you are dispelling the illusion, which means your focus is now on abundance.

Reaffirm your new beliefs daily because this is your self-contract, so you must hold yourself accountable.

When you write down a positive statement about yourself, you make it physical, which gives it life. This applies to affirmations, intentions, goals, and dreams.

ACTION STEP 3: To change your beliefs, you must change who you are. You are not your shadow side; your past experiences and false beliefs just make you lose sight of the fact that *you are a child of God with unlimited potential, resources, and abilities*. When you see the real you, you will have absolute power to create the life you desire.

The subconscious mind believes what you tell it; it doesn't know the difference between real and imagined. Therefore, what you believe is your reality. When you no longer resonate with your false beliefs and you refuse to believe that there are any limitations, you will create a new neural pathway to abundance. By adopting abundant beliefs, you rewire the subconscious mind to deliver positive results.

ACTION STEP 4: Release the emotions associated with your false beliefs.

False beliefs foster feelings of unworthiness and inadequacy, but remember they are just an illusion. You can choose not to let those feelings affect you by embodying the real you, which is the spirit of abundance.

You can begin to embrace abundance by generating feelings of gratitude, contentment, and fulfillment in all areas of your life. As a result, a sense of wholeness will take root and become your new normal.

ACTION STEP 5: Practice your new beliefs daily by taking action to prove that they're real. This means demonstrating acts of abundance.

For example, you could practice gratitude, follow your dreams and aspirations, buy a cup of coffee for the person behind you in the drive-through, help someone in need, give compliments, notice the magic in everyday moments, say "thank you" more, meditate, set a positive intention for the day, make a list of things you'd like to accomplish and then accomplish them, etc. Being abundant is acting beyond the norm; it's a demonstration that your cup runneth over.

ACTION STEP 6: Your daily thoughts, words, feelings, visions, and actions must be congruent with abundance. When you are in alignment and you remain consistent, you are working toward one goal and one outcome.

Think of all the successful athletes in the world. What do they all have in common? Repetition and alignment. They train day in and day out because they understand that they must align their priorities with their goals in order to achieve the results they desire. They are not deterred by their moods, the weather, or faulty beliefs. They show up for themselves. You can do the same by retraining your mind to focus on abundance.

It's essential to adopt abundant beliefs and good habits because you become what you believe and what you repeatedly do. We will discuss abundant beliefs in more detail later in this chapter.

Think of the subconscious mind as a software program. Tech companies frequently release new and improved versions, adding more benefits and features. Your belief system requires the same reset because the program that runs in your mind is your reality. When you upgrade your beliefs, you upgrade your life.

Conversely, when you don't know your worth, you attract experiences that trigger your fears and insecurities. For example, we've all experienced those wonderful people who love to push our buttons. They say something or do something that makes us feel frustrated, angry, or hurt, causing us to act out of character.

When this happens, pause and reflect. Self-reflection allows you to analyze and determine why a person's behavior upsets you. Many times, you will find that the experiences you attract reveal the beliefs you have about yourself.

Become an investigator, digging deep to uncover your false beliefs. Did the experience make you feel unappreciated or unloved? Did it make you feel unworthy? Did it make you feel misunderstood? Did it make you feel rejected or humiliated? Did it make you feel betrayed or deceived?

Some experiences undermine your self-confidence and chip away at your self-esteem, but the reality is that internalizing what people say means you're giving meaning and value to their words. *The people in your life hold up a mirror to you, shining a light on who you are.* Through their words and actions, they reflect to you how you see yourself and how you feel about yourself, thereby reinforcing your beliefs.

Think back to a time when someone made fun of you or belittled you with their words. When you accept someone's disparaging remarks, you're affirming or reaffirming a false belief that you are inadequate. You'll continue to have similar experiences until you learn the truth: *you lack nothing*. But it's with each experience that you begin to uncover your self-imposed limitations, leading to a change in perspective and belief. It is through self-realization that the veil is lifted to show you who you really are: valuable, abundant, and limitless.

I was in my midtwenties when I noticed the universe letting me in on a secret: it was listening to me. I would ask questions, and answers would come to me through a thought, a book, or a message. I'd see a sign, like a sequence of numbers, or I'd receive an experience that reaffirmed how I felt about myself.

I realized that whether or not you consciously seek guidance, the universe responds to you. It matches and returns the vibration of who you are—your self-concept, beliefs, and feelings. For example, if you feel discontent and resentful over another's achievements or possessions, the projection of your beliefs and feelings will provide you with experiences that make you envious until you recognize your actions are motivated by envy.

What is envy? It's believing that you cannot have what others have. What's the cause of this behavior? A false belief of being inferior. Envy, like other negative emotions, is the result of identifying with fear instead of love, which leads to a scarcity mindset and a deflated self-concept. Consequently, you feel unworthy of what you desire because you don't know your worth.

Your experiences periodically remind you of where you are in your journey, what you need to learn about yourself, and what you need to work on to get where you are meant to be.

With this knowledge in mind, let's study ourselves now and figure out the limitations that we have unknowingly placed on ourselves. By eliminating our false beliefs, we can reprogram our minds to deliver positive results. Otherwise, we'll remain on autopilot, allowing our subconscious minds to attract challenging scenarios that trigger our self-limiting thoughts, insecurities, and fears.

Each one of us is responsible for this vehicle God gave us, which includes our mind, body, and spirit. We tend to focus on healthy eating and exercise, but eliminating false beliefs is equally essential in every area of our lives.

For instance, whenever someone has an obsession or a feeling of possessiveness over another person, it's because they're tying their worth to the other party, which means they haven't identified with love for self. When you believe you need another person to feel loved, secure, and happy, you unknowingly live in fear of loss and abandonment, which creates resistance and prevents you from getting the results you desire. This emotional reliance on a partner is codependency.

If you rely on a person, what happens if they decide to break up with you? Do you fall to pieces and wait for their return to put yourself back together? That sounds silly, right? But when you lack self-love, it's because you don't know your worth, which causes you to become dependent on another for your mental and emotional stability. This false belief that your worth comes from the attention you receive from others results in behavioral patterns like being needy, having emotional outbursts, seeking validation, being controlling, wanting others to rescue you, and putting people on a pedestal. This type of behavior exhibits a lack of self-love due to a belief that your worth is found outside of you.

To overcome this false belief, you must know your value comes from within. Your beliefs control your inner voice, which either builds you up or breaks you down. Therefore, you must have abundant beliefs in place, so you're connected to a healthy self-image. When you build a solid foundation of love within yourself, you hold yourself in high regard. It's then that you no longer feel helpless in the face of others' actions.

Your self-worth is not determined by who is standing by your side; it's determined by your self-concept. Therefore, you must be self-sufficient and know you're whole on your own. A significant other should complement you, bring out the best in you, and add to the love you already have for yourself. The truth is, the love you need is within you, but sometimes you need life lessons to realize that you are complete within yourself.

Your beliefs determine the relationships you attract, how far you advance in life, and what you think about. What happens when you think about something over and over again, give it meaning, and accept it as true? You either reinforce a belief or create a new belief that becomes your reality. To rise higher, you must break free from the false beliefs and conditioning that made you who you think you are. That's right: who you *think* you are, not who you really are.

Who you *really* are is your Higher Self, abundant in every way. Ask yourself, *Am I going to continue to live my life based on outdated beliefs that no longer serve me, or am I going to take charge of my life and align with beliefs that serve my highest good?*

A false belief is just a story you continue to tell yourself and believe to be true. How do you want to live? Who do you want to become? You have to let go of the illusions to create the future that you desire, and it starts with adopting abundant beliefs.

Abundant Beliefs

Imagine that within you there is an overflowing treasure chest filled with an infinite supply of abundance. It never runs out. When you need something, you go within and select it—and the best part? It's free.

You have access to abundance twenty-four hours a day, seven days a week. Abundant living is knowing you are fully stocked because of God's presence within you.

Luke 17:21 (King James Version) states, "The kingdom of God is within you." Think about how powerful this verse is. *God works through us, and our riches lie within.* When you recognize your divinity and act as one with God in spirit, you step into your fullness. You live in the divine light, knowing that all things are possible with God.

John 14:6 (KJV) states, "Jesus saith unto him, I am the way, the truth, and the life: no man cometh unto the Father, but by me." What does this verse mean? My interpretation is that the way to God is through alignment with Christ Consciousness, which emanates from your Higher Self.

What is the Higher Self? It's a state of living in which you cultivate Christlike attributes: faith in God, unconditional love, self-awareness, kindness, acceptance, honesty, respect, authenticity, oneness, creativity, nonresistance, nonjudgment, generosity, intuition, compassion, forgiveness, humility, patience, and trust in yourself and your abilities. It's characterized by having an abundance mindset, living in the here and now, and exercising your will as a co-creator with God.

Matthew 6:33 (KJV) states, "But seek ye first the kingdom of God, and his righteousness; and all these things shall be added unto you." This verse speaks of obeying divine law—that is, being a good steward of God by living in the vibration of love and having high moral values. The radiant energy Christ displayed on earth is the state of abundance. With this knowledge in mind, let's follow the leader so that we can rise in Christ Consciousness. Remember, your reality merely reflects the energy you project; you get back from the universe what you put out.

When you are pure of heart and have high moral values, you act out of love for yourself, love for others, and love for your dreams and aspirations. You understand the Golden Rule: treat others as you would like to be treated.

When you're aligned with your Higher Self, you are consciously aware of your behavior, which means the light stays on 24/7. You manage your mental, emotional, and spiritual realities to create the physical reality that you desire. You realize no one else is like you; your essence is unique. You understand that the reason you are here is to expand your soul and become a higher version of yourself through self-realization, self-awareness, open-mindedness, authenticity, knowledge, good works, and living in the vibration of love.

Each of us has a purpose, and knowledge of this truth is your power, for your existence plays an important role in the grand design of the universe. You were born to make an impact on the world and the people in your life. Your mission is important because every soul's actions affect humanity and the collective consciousness.

With this knowledge in mind, why on earth would we ever question ourselves or our abilities? When we don't acknowledge God's presence within us, understand the importance of love for self and others, know our worth, and follow our soul's purpose, we deny our power and block our blessings. By unknowingly edging God out, we lead with the ego, the lower self. What is the role of the ego? It summons its fake friends to come out and play—fear, worry, and doubt, to name a few.

Insecurities are nothing more than false beliefs triggering fear to come to the surface. Instead, let's allow love to surface so that we come from a place of empowerment, for we are sitting on a gold mine of divine intelligence, innate tools, and abundance. What's holding us back? A lack of action. Nothing can grow and evolve in life without movement.

It's up to us to make every moment count. So let's begin by unearthing the hidden treasure that lies within. Life is abundant when you are actively loving, learning, creating, giving, playing, growing, and evolving. Life is the process of birthing your desires.

We are creative beings—works of art. When you use your creative energy to paint your reality, you reveal the uniqueness of your soul. What is your uniqueness? It's your contribution to society—the expression of your talents, skills, and abilities. It's also your story, the experiences you've had, and the knowledge and wisdom you've gained along the way. These gifts benefit all of humankind.

When you realize you are whole, you become abundant. You radiate faith, belief, and hope because you are living in the vibration of love. In contrast, when you feel that you need someone, don't have enough of something, or are afraid to step into the unknown, you project your incompleteness into the universe and resist the truth of wholeness—thus refuting your desires. Again, a scarcity mindset radiates fear-based energy.

If you believe you are unworthy of your desires, go within, uproot this false belief, and replace it with the truth: abundance is your birthright. You must demonstrate you are abundant by making choices and decisions that serve your highest good and the greater good. This includes strengthening your mind, body, and spirit; being grateful; following your dreams and aspirations; being of service; and offering a product or service to the world.

An abundant belief is an unseen action that works behind the scenes to get the ball rolling. It's your most powerful tool because it's a thought, a choice, a decision, a feeling, a vision, and an action, all aligned to deliver the same powerful outcome: the truth of existence. Your beliefs attract your desires when you believe them to be true in your mind, feel them to be real in your heart, and use your divine will to enable action to bring them to life; your mind, emotions, and will must be in harmony.

For example, when you place an order online, you pay for it and expect it to be delivered. You know it's on its way, so you remain steadfast, satisfied, and assured. The same behavior applies to your dreams; when you place your order with the universe, you must act as if what you're asking for has already been fulfilled. You must remain nonresistant, committed to riding the tide of life, not swimming against it.

Where there is a peaceful heart and mind, there is trust, faith, belief, gratitude, contentment, fulfillment, and an enlightened perspective. *That* is abundance. The key is to become the vibration of what you desire, which is adopting the feeling that it already exists. You must then demonstrate that certainty through your daily actions, turning it into reality.

However, before you can embark on this epic adventure, you must become the captain of your ship. You will need to figure out the coordinates of your destination before you leave the port. Where are you going? How are you getting there?

What's the purpose, intention, and motivating factor of your journey?

When you begin your voyage, you must remain at the helm in a conscious state of mind so that you can steer your ship in the right direction. You must stay the course by remaining rooted in your desires, knowing that your dreams will come to fruition through dedication and discipline. You can't question this truth, doubt it, or give up, and you can't wonder if or when your manifestation will arrive. You must know that what you're asking for is already yours. It always has been and always will be because you've declared it so.

Above all, don't forget to wear your life jacket at all times, because you will need it. If you haven't already guessed, that life jacket is God. You will need him because there will be storms along the way and the water may be choppy at times, but rest assured, God's got you. Live by faith, stand by your beliefs, don't get overwhelmed by obstacles and delays, and no matter what, always keep moving forward.

When you bring your dreams and aspirations into focus, the universe guides you by illuminating all the things you need to learn, know, understand, and overcome. For example, you may realize you should take a class to sharpen your skills, or you might make mistakes that cause you to become more knowledgeable.

The universe will also send you signs and synchronicities to communicate with you and keep you balanced, motivated, and in the right state of mind. You will receive number sequences and messages from family members, friends, random strangers, or animals crossing your path, as well as through vivid dreams, objects, books, articles, songs, advertisements, etc. When you believe in your desires, act in faith, and match the vibration of your future reality, you will be divinely led by the universe. Why? Because you are acting as one with God, the builder of all things.

Consider your dreams to be on spiritual layaway, where belief is the deposit and your desires are earned through your performance. You can't live the life you desire until you match the vibration of what you desire. Therefore, you have to embody your dream by becoming the person with the right attitude, habits, skills, knowledge, experience, and more. Every day is an opportunity to turn your life into everything you want it to be, but first, you have to prepare to receive it and then trust in divine timing.

What does your life look like? Is it blooming in all seasons? Your life is like a garden; it requires your undivided attention to thrive. To live an abundant life, you must plant rich beliefs, which are the seeds of greatness, and uproot the false beliefs that are nothing more than weeds trying to overrun the mind. Abundant beliefs take root when you become an expression of them through your thoughts, words, feelings, and actions, which leads to a bountiful harvest.

Here are some positive affirmations that align with God's frequency—Christ Consciousness, your Higher Self: "As I speak, the right people and opportunities are entering my life, and they are blessings from God. I am an expression of unconditional love and abundance. I am grateful for everything I have and for the opportunity to create, grow, and evolve."

Before you recite your affirmations aloud, align yourself with the vibration of abundance, which is gratitude, contentment, and fulfillment. This practice makes you feel whole, and when you feel whole, your words become powerful, taking on meaning, value, and life. When you repeat them often, form a mental image of your new identity, and take action, you're making an impression on the subconscious mind that this is *who you are*. Your beliefs become valid when your words, thoughts, feelings, vision, and actions align.

Here's an affirmation script that will encourage, motivate, and challenge you to live an abundant life:

> "I am one with God in spirit; therefore, I am the divine designer of my destiny. I get up before the sun rises every day and start each day with prayer and gratitude. Every night before my head hits the pillow, I end each day with prayer and gratitude, having envisioned the next day's events. I laugh, have fun, and spend quality time with the people I love. I am generous, kind, and thoughtful, and I inspire others with my words and actions. I attract limitless abundance into all areas of my life because I am abundant. I am healthy, happy, and prosperous, and I have a wise and discerning mind. My energy radiates peace because it emanates from the light. I live in faith, and I see, speak, and act out of love. My mindset is that of an eagle, allowing me to soar to new heights. I am bold, confident, and courageous, and I conquer all feats big and small. I live a purpose-driven life, and my attention is focused on positive actions that take me higher. I balance my emotions,

challenge myself, and hold myself accountable for my actions. I am disciplined and
practice self-control. I have good habits, exercise, eat nourishing foods, and enjoy all the
good things life has to offer. I will treat this
day and every day as the blessing it is."

Recite this affirmation script three times a day for ninety
days; that's how long it typically takes to create a new lifestyle.
Infuse your words with heartfelt emotion, form a mental image of your new self, and practice what you preach so it becomes your reality.

Your beliefs determine your quality of life because your
belief system is your self-concept, which becomes the paradigm of your habitual behavior—the fixed pattern of how you
think and act. Therefore, you will only go in life where you
believe you can go, and you will only get out of life what you
believe you are worthy of receiving.

So imagine what a shock it is to your paradigm when you
decide to venture out of your comfort zone while still har-
boring false beliefs. It throws up a red flag via your thoughts
and emotions, causing you to stop dead in your tracks. This is
when you begin to question yourself, asking, *Am I making the
right decision? Is this a good idea?* If this happens, it's a clear sign
that you need to clean house because your paradigm should
say, "Go for it!"

Reprogramming a paradigm is like breaking a bad habit.
You have to be willing to reinvent yourself, to change the way
you see, think, and feel about yourself because your self-concept determines your behavior.

ACTION STEP 1: Set an intention to live an abundant life.

For example: "From this day forward, I am living life to the fullest because I am on God's path creating an abundant life."

ACTION STEP 2: Change your self-concept.

Remember, your self-concept is who you believe you are and what you believe you're capable of achieving. So, you must see the real you, not the version created by your past experiences.

ACTION STEP 3: Raise your standards. Define what your highest quality of life is (e.g., a healthy mind/body/spirit, a loving partnership, and a peaceful and fulfilling life).

How are you going to achieve this high-quality life? Create an action plan detailing what you need to do—what you need to change about yourself and your life—because your standards, habits, and routines create your reality.

ACTION STEP 4: Establish an abundance mindset by weeding out the thoughts that do not serve you.

To change your inner voice, practice positive self-talk and affirmations daily. When you influence your subconscious mind through repetition, your words will soon register, resulting in new beliefs and a new self-image.

ACTION STEP 5: Live in a state of gratitude.

When you're thankful for what you have, you are given more reasons to be grateful. Gratitude is the vibration of abundance.

ACTION STEP 6: Act as if you are abundant.

The more acts of abundance you exhibit, the more you will experience abundance, because you're leaving impressions of your new reality on the subconscious mind. It's a game of follow-the-leader; you must be the leader to reprogram your mind.

When you see yourself as being whole and you think, feel, and act abundantly, the universe mirrors you, and you are rewarded with the fullness of life. To maintain that life, however, you must replace fear with faith.

CHAPTER 2

FEAR AND FAITH

It was my freshman year when the classroom door opened and my teacher was handed a note that was then passed to me. The note read, "Please report to the office."

What was this about? Immediately, I started to question myself. *Did I do something wrong? Why do they want to see me?*

As I entered the office, I was filled with fear and insecurity. A school official asked, "Did your family move out of town?" When I replied yes, they responded, "You can no longer attend this school because you are living outside of the school district."

Once again, I felt like I didn't belong. Did I attract this experience into my life? Of course I did. I was fearful they would find out the truth, and my fears and beliefs returned to sender.

Do you see the recurring patterns and repercussions that play out when you have false beliefs and live in fear-based energy? You continue to attract experiences that magnify them until you realize through self-awareness and self-realization that they are nothing more than an illusion.

Growing up, I didn't want anyone to know that my family was facing financial instability. I was worried about superficial things like my image, and I didn't want to be looked down upon—but that's exactly what I was doing to myself. Unknowingly, I was conditioning myself to feel insecure and unworthy because that is what I focused on, projected, and believed to be true.

If I could turn back time and talk to my younger self, I would say, "Stop comparing yourself to others. God made you in his image, so hold on to that image. Move forward with confidence, seeing yourself the way God sees you. Know that your past experiences do not define you; instead, you extract the lessons from them. Your self-concept defines you. So don't diminish your value with faulty thinking and fear-based emotions. Rise up, know your worth, love yourself, and walk in faith."

I'm still learning and growing, but now I have the awareness that you can choose either fear or faith. Fear leaves you feeling helpless, hopeless, stressed, worried, and overwhelmed, which is living life with the light off, whereas faith takes you to a wonderful place of love, hope, optimism, peace, joy, happiness, and excitement about life because you're living in a state of wholeness. Both of these beliefs are invisible to the naked eye, but the one you choose to believe in determines whether you create heaven or hell in your reality.

For instance, if you believe it's hard to make money, or that money is the root of all evil, you will always be chasing after it. Why? Because those are disempowering, fear-based beliefs that create resistance to receiving. Therefore, you must believe that money is a positive, helpful, and generous gift from the universe. As we've discussed, your mindset and vibration are a magnet, so you must imagine, feel, and believe that abundance is coming to you 24/7 in all aspects of your life: health, family, relationships, fitness, career, finances, etc.

Why is a high vibration needed when manifesting? *Because love is the divine energy of creation—the element that brings your dreams and aspirations to life.* When your focus is on creating, your energy is in building mode, which means you are transferring the emotion of love into your desires.

Living in the present moment is the key to creating an abundant life, because you are consciously aware of your mood, daily habits, and actions, allowing you to live with intention—whereas living on autopilot is being unmindful and predictable, following a monotonous cycle, and not making a decision to alter it, which keeps you from progressing.

That being said, you have the power to flip the script and alchemize your energy. You get to choose whether you are going to shrink with fear or expand with faith.

Fear

You can count on fear to make itself known when you decide to venture out of your comfort zone. That's when the self-defeating inner voice rises to say, "Hey, are you sure we should do this? Maybe we should just stay put." It sees the unknown as a threat and tells you to live in your safely managed world, where you may not be entirely happy but at least you don't have to do much more than what you're currently doing. In this controllable state, you don't have to upset the apple cart and find out what's on the other side of fear.

Fear is a signal to protect you from physical harm; it's a survival mechanism. It was not designed to stop you from fulfilling your dreams. Because fear is the energy of false beliefs, it creates an illusionary roadblock that serves up self-limiting thoughts about why you shouldn't take action. This state of mind can prevent you from moving forward, because your energy has created a self-imposed obstacle that thwarts your will.

At other times, fear can be a catalyst for a big change that you don't want to make, and it won't leave you alone until you face it. Then, it disappears. That is the purpose of fear: through an intense feeling of discomfort, it shines an inner light on your false beliefs so that you are aware of them and can eliminate them and move forward.

It's important to let fear highlight your insecurities so that you can identify your false beliefs, but don't allow it to foster negativity. If you do, fear can become your inner bully—controlling your mind, making you doubt yourself, and causing procrastination and irrational thinking.

If you lack the self-confidence and certainty to make a change, know that your energy has shifted from love to fear. When you allow that fear to manipulate and misguide you, you're living through your ego and not your Higher Self. So, don't allow fear to decide your fate. Instead, convert fear into faith by changing your perspective and seeing the value in deciding to act. Ask yourself, *How is this change going to benefit me?* When you see change as a catalyst for progress and transformation, you transmute your vibration from negative to positive. This paradigm shift empowers you to embrace the unknown with greater clarity, complete confidence, and acts of courage, demonstrating your inner strength.

I believe many fear the unknown because there are no guarantees. If you want reassurance that you are making the right decision, it's a sign that you don't believe in yourself and that you lack faith. But when you acknowledge your divinity, you are aligned with the solid foundation that God has laid before you. You walk with confidence, unshaken by the unknown, because you understand that each of us has been given the title of co-creator, along with a set of innate tools for designing an abundant life—free, compliments of God. Luke 12:48 (KJV) states, "For unto whomsoever much is given, of him shall be much required." This verse speaks to the importance of putting our God-given talents and abilities to good use.

But how many of us are actively creating positive changes in our lives? Why do we shy away from doing so? Why do we look at the unknown as a threat? Why do we underestimate our abilities and diminish our light?

Greatness lies within, but it's up to us to express it. When you are one with God in spirit, live by faith, and use your inner tools, you are a limitless being. *What are these tools?* They are reason, imagination, intuition, memory, perception, and will—the six intelligences of the mind. We will discuss how to use these higher mental faculties in the final chapter of this book.

Once again, don't allow fear to stop you, and don't allow it to take over. Instead, relish change, embrace it, and take a leap of faith because this is your opportunity to advance. When you do what's right for you, not what's easy, you make bold moves and think optimistically—because you understand that your life will only be as interesting as you make it.

Sometimes, people fear change because they don't want to make a mistake, but mistakes allow you to learn what works and what doesn't. They cause you to reflect, they allow you to be innovative, they get your creative juices flowing, and they sharpen the mind through the use of your critical thinking skills (e.g., question, interpret, analyze, evaluate). We tend to think of mistakes as misfortune, but on the contrary, they are blessings in disguise because they are learning opportunities that help us become more knowledgeable.

When you believe in yourself and your abilities, you're in alignment with your Higher Self, which means you rise above the ego's fears—mistakes, risk, failure, and looking foolish in the eyes of others. Taking a leap of faith is about creating your best life rather than letting fear hold you back. If you are worried about failing, know that the only way to fail is to give up, stop, and not continue to take action. However, winning is a part of our DNA. Therefore, we must apply ourselves until we reach the finish line. God designed us to be finishers—to accomplish our tasks and to inspire others to do the same—because we are a reflection of him.

Still, when you go after your dreams, you will become your own worst critic. You will second guess yourself, doubts will creep in, your self-confidence will drop, and you will try to talk yourself out of continuing. Why? Because pursuing your dreams takes time. When what you envisioned doesn't happen overnight, you will want to give up, but you should expect that creating the life of your dreams will be more work than you first anticipated. Dreams require your full attention; therefore, you must spare no effort and be willing to make personal sacrifices.

When you enter uncharted territory, you must also be prepared to face challenges, which can cause you to feel frustrated and uneasy at times. But know that challenges come when the rewards are greater; they are growing pains. Problems, delays, and obstacles are temporary; the tide always turns. There is always a solution to a problem. An obstacle makes you shift your perspective, and delays deliberately buy you more time to make what you're working on even better.

The short-term discomfort you experience when faced with challenges has long-term benefits, as this process of character development makes you into the person you need to be to achieve your goals. That's why the journey is far greater than the reward you will receive: it's the *journey* that makes you greater than you are now. You will find the real reward is in the brilliant bits of wisdom you gain along the way. Growth broadens the mind, and you can't put a price on gaining a heightened level of awareness, new knowledge, and new insights. These valuable gifts can only be acquired through your performance.

But know that you can only create positive change when your energy is at peace, not war. When you are anxious, worried, frustrated, and stressed, that's the ego stepping in, which creates fear and resistance and closes the door to abundance.

The ego will not tell you to go inward and change what you're thinking about, so you can shift your vibration back to love; rather, its focus is on the outside world's perceptions because it's the energy of fear, which is a lack of awareness of your divinity. The ego is an illusion of separation, and as such, it's afraid of the unknown. Its self-image feels threatened by others, so when it's challenged, it will defend its self-imposed limitations. It also possesses negative human traits. The ego believes it's a one-man show and can't imagine relinquishing control. It doesn't live in the present moment; it's too busy living in the past or worrying about the future. It wears a mask to hide its insecurities and protect its image. It's self-absorbed, prideful, vain, materialistic, narcissistic, greedy, selfish, sarcastic, vindictive, jealous, deceptive, impatient, reactionary, impulsive, irrational, condescending, competitive, entitled, reckless, ruthless, rude, and resistant. It blocks out intuition, creates division, makes assumptions, promotes negative thinking, feels discontent, cares about what others think, and makes you question yourself. As if that were not enough, it also wants to be recognized and rewarded by the outside world.

You reap your rewards by rising to become one with your Higher Self because you are more than an earthbound physical body. You are a spiritual being having a human experience for the evolution of your soul. Your Higher Self has awareness because it's in alignment with God, which means there are no boundaries, no limitations, and no need for validation. Why? Because you are fully aware that the spark of the divine lives within you, making you a beacon of light, which allows you to create the life you desire from the inside out.

Your Higher Self is where your power lies, as self-realization of your divinity, self-awareness of your actions, and the conscious choice to create positive change free you from fear. This state allows you to live a life driven by faith, focus, purpose, and intention, leading to freedom, abundance, and infinite opportunities. By deflating the ego and exuding humility, the Higher Self also exhibits unconditional love and nonresistance, free from judgment and attachment. Psalm 37:11 (KJV) states, "But the meek shall inherit the earth; and shall delight themselves in the abundance of peace."

Your vibration determines your quality of life. So why on earth would we give fear the time of day when we know that abundance comes from living in the light? Fear may weigh heavily on you at times, but know that it holds no value. The more attention you give to fear, the more energy you feed it. The way to stop fear dead in its tracks is to take away its supply. It's powerless without your energy, so instead, give your energy to faith.

Faith

I grew up with a strong belief in God. My parents ignited the fire of faith within me, and the hardships I've faced in life have brought me closer to God.

What is faith? Faith is the act of surrendering your desires to God because you are certain of his existence. It's having confidence that what you're working on will come to pass. It's trusting that God has plans to prosper you and give you hope, no matter what you're currently going through.

Living by faith is the state of wholeness because you are aligned with God's will. Your faith, coupled with a close relationship with God, cultivates a mindset and vibration that reflect love, gratitude, contentment, and fulfillment. It's through this alignment that we become receptive to his many blessings.

Having faith is understanding that life is happening for you; changes, challenges, delays, obstacles, struggles, and suffering are here to educate and elevate you. Therefore, you must maintain a positive attitude, so you can remain on God's path of unity, balance, and progression.

If you want to discover how to live your best life, look to nature; it's your teacher. Just as the sun peeks through the clouds, making you feel better, you can always go within to change an emotionally cloudy day into a sunny day. Just as the trees don't uproot and run away during a storm, you can stand in your power, rooted in faith and nonresistant to the winds of pressure. Nature is cyclical, and so is life. There will be seasons of joy and seasons of challenges. If you follow nature's nonresistance to change and transformation, you will thrive.

Following your dreams requires the same mental toughness. You have to remain rooted in your desires to make them your reality. You must go all in. The only way to truly guarantee success is to believe that your current course of action is the only course of action. When you shake off fear and wear God's mighty armor of belief, courage, and confidence, you walk in faith.

Think back to when you were a kid and your parents told you to go play. You wouldn't think twice about it—you would just do it because you trusted them. We should have the same faith in God, our Heavenly Father.

Picture God saying, "Trust me: I've got this. I received your request through your power of belief. Now, go have fun and enjoy this beautiful day!" How would you feel? You would most likely feel loved, protected, happy, and free to enjoy life. That's the all-encompassing vibration of trust that leads to the fulfillment of your desires. It's the art of letting go of control.

Whenever you feel fearful, stop and remember who you are and where you came from, so you can rise and return to wholeness. When you move through life with fearless faith, determined to reach your goals, you become an attractor—a magnet to your desires—because you're vibrating in love. You just have to trust in divine timing and take action. Faith in good works is an act of God.

Do you think God worries? No. Do you think God lets fear keep him from deciding to act? Of course not. God doesn't live in fear.

God made us in his image, so why do we live in fear? Why do we worry? Why do we doubt ourselves? When you let go of fear and choose to experience life through love, you become one with God. 1 John 4:16 (KJV) states, "God is love; and he that dwelleth in love dwelleth in God, and God in him."

However, God gave us free will. We get to choose if we'd rather question our abilities, complain, and live in fear, uncertainty, complacency, and stagnation, producing more of the same old mundane routines and challenging experiences. Or, we can become pillars of light through love, faith, belief, and inspired action.

God created the universe, and it has divine order. The Law of Cause and Effect states that the energy you put out, you get back. With this in mind, let's generate positive energy by rising above our current circumstances, turning our back on fear, walking in faith, and making changes that match our heart's desires. Let's become victors, knowing that there is a greater purpose in life: to prosper and to be a channel for God's love.

CHAPTER 3

EMOTIONS

One day when I was in my forties, I was lying on the couch, facing the darkness of the cushions. I couldn't bear to look at the external world because I didn't want to face what was going on in my life.

I wasn't being my authentic self. I was gay, but others didn't know because I was keeping it to myself. By choosing to live in fear, I created a self-imposed mental prison, where I caused myself unnecessary stress.

At that time, I didn't know how to move forward because I was at war with my thoughts and emotions, which kept me in a low vibration. I was not loving myself, and for that reason alone, I was not in a good place mentally or emotionally.

As in earlier times in my life, I just wanted to fit in, so I let false beliefs and fear-based emotions drive my life. I put the thoughts of others' opinions and reactions above my own happiness. I painted an undesirable picture in my mind, believed it to be true, and lived in despair. By not changing my perspective, I surrendered my power, which put me in survival mode.

Survival mode occurs when a stressful life event, such as a loss or trauma, emotionally triggers you and robs you of your peace of mind. This is when you proceed on autopilot, going through the motions of life without enthusiasm instead of creating the life you desire.

When you're in survival mode, you create suffering, because you think things will not get better, due to a false belief that what you are facing is insurmountable. With this hopeless mindset, you continue to live in worry, grief, or other fear-based emotions, resulting in an emotional burden.

When difficulties arise, where does your attention go? To the problem. When you're focused on a negative outcome, you can adopt an unsatisfactory attitude toward the situation, which causes a mental block. Why does this happen? Because you are no longer in the driver's seat, which means you are not consciously aware of your actions. You are solely focused on how you are feeling and the new reality you're facing; you're not living in the present moment, because your focus has shifted to what happened in the past or what might happen in the future.

If you feel you are in over your head, you must become an observer, because negative thoughts and emotions cloud your judgment. You must ask yourself, *How can I look at what I am going through differently, so I can shift my perspective and get myself in a better place both mentally and emotionally?*

When you change your perception, you change your reality. Granted, the circumstances may remain the same, but by shifting your perspective, you can see the situation in a whole new light. This change of attitude allows you to accept what you're going through, so you can continue to move forward. It's through rational thinking, faith, and positive forward movement that life gets better.

Traumatic life events can be very stressful, but you always have a choice regarding how you manage your emotions. We tend to feel our way through life, but it takes logical thinking to return to a positive state of being. Inner conflict is self-generated; when you take time to reflect on your actions, you can see how negative thoughts and emotions trick your mind into believing something is real when it isn't.

We all face challenging situations from time to time, but it's up to us to take responsibility for our mental, emotional, and physical health. Whenever you feel overwhelmed by a situation, know that this too shall pass and the sun will shine again. Something that works for me is to surrender the situation to God, which releases resistance and restores peace and harmony, providing freedom from fixation, obsession, worry, anger, or sadness.

When you live in fear, you separate yourself from love, and love is home. That's why fear makes you feel lost, uneasy, empty, and all alone: because you've wandered away from who you really are, where you came from, and where you belong. But there is a gift that comes from adversity; struggle, hardships, and challenging times reveal to you just how strong you are. These experiences also provide a deeper level of awareness and valuable insights to help you navigate through life.

When you are self-aware, you oversee your energy by keeping the power on twenty-four hours a day, seven days a week, through emotional intelligence, movement, creativity, and gratitude.

Emotional Intelligence

Because we tend to spend most of our time on autopilot, we have to practice being consciously aware of our actions. By self-regulating first thing in the morning, you can create a healthy daily routine that supports positive thinking. When you direct your mind, rather than your subconscious mind leading you, you can empower yourself mentally and emotionally to create a productive and successful day.

On the other end of the spectrum, when you're not consciously aware of your behavior, you can fall victim to your environment, letting your emotions control you. In this state, you react emotionally to others' comments, what you see on the news, and the minutiae of everyday life.

What's the difference between reacting and responding? Reacting is leading with your emotions, while responding is using logic over emotion. When you respond, you think before you act, which means you are aware of the consequences of your behavior. Therefore, you act intuitively, strategically, and intentionally, rather than impulsively.

For example, let's say you are on the treadmill listening to music and your earbuds stop working. A second ago, you were in a good mood with a pep in your step. Now, you are in silence with your thoughts. What are you thinking? *I should have charged them before I went to the gym. What am I going to do now, work out for another thirty minutes in silence? Maybe I should just stop.* When the earbuds died, so did the power within.

Why does this negative transformation happen? Because your feelings are the physical result of what you've been thinking and believing. Emotions are felt in the body, and they reveal your mood, which then dictates your actions if you allow it to.

For example, what if you wake up in the morning and are feeling down because of a recent breakup? Or, what if you are upset because you argued with your spouse the night before? What if you're dreading going back to the office because the workload is overwhelming? When you are in your feelings, it's because you made what you're going through your main focus, the most important thing, and you gave it meaning, which affirms a belief. It's the belief that allows you to feel the emotion related to the experience, such as sadness, worry, or grief—which, in turn, becomes your reality.

However, when you don't become emotionally invested—when you choose not to identify with the outcome of a situation as the be-all and end-all—it's an act of self-love. That self-love allows you to change your perspective and remain positive, thus putting you in charge of the day's events.

Creating a harmonious life requires emotional stability. To make yourself feel better, you must change what you are thinking and believing, because change begins in the mind. When you have a positive mindset, your energy is nonresistant. You don't live on a roller-coaster ride, where your emotions take you up and down from day to day based on the weather, what's going on in the world, what someone said to you, or what's happening at work. You keep your mood meter set on abundance, which puts you in harmony with creating and receiving what you desire.

Having emotional intelligence means being aware of your feelings and being able to filter out the self-defeating thoughts that do not serve you—thoughts like *I can't go on without you* or *You are the only one for me.* These examples show how false beliefs can cause emotional blockages. When you don't allow your emotions to flow through you, you tell yourself the same story over and over—and it's not even a good story.

If you find yourself feeling defeated, ask yourself, *Why did I attract this experience into my life? How did my thoughts, beliefs, and behavior contribute to this event?* It's okay for us to sit in our emotions to make an observation because we need to learn from the experience and work through it. But it doesn't do us any good to resist reality by remaining rooted in low vibrational energy; it only creates unnecessary stress.

Whenever you feel anxious or depressed, think about what's playing out in your mind and whether you've created a false narrative. When you are not aware of your behavior, you can continue to sit in a despondent state. For example, when you feel depressed, you may be thinking of a past event that made you feel hopeless, or you could be sad because you're not happy with your current reality and you don't believe things will get better. When you feel anxious, you may be replaying a stressful or traumatic event that took place in the past or projecting an imaginary fear that you believe will take place in the future.

It's not easy to put your feelings aside, but you are the only one who can change your state of mind. Ask yourself, *What good is it doing me to hold on to these emotions, if they are not making me feel good?*

It's not healthy to sit in a negative emotional state, because this behavior can block your progress and affect your well-being and quality of life. For example, when you create a strong belief that something will happen but the outcome doesn't work out in your favor, you may feel discontentment, disappointment, sadness, or hopelessness, and these emotions can make you resistant to change. If you don't accept a situation for what it is and move on, your negative thoughts and feelings will create a future without joy, because your focus lies on negativity. But when you make peace with the present moment and don't wish it to be different, you detach from your emotions and become nonresistant, which brings you back to a state of wholeness.

Look for the lesson in every challenging situation you go through so that you can level up. Trust that when things don't go your way, the experience is serving your highest good. It's in the disappointments and emotional breakdowns that we receive *breakthroughs* of awareness to wake us up to the true nature of a situation. As we've discussed, challenges bring growth, redirection, wisdom, and better opportunities.

Living in low vibrational energy is an act of self-sabotage. If you're experiencing something that is causing inner conflict, remove your judgment of it so that you can release the burden. Judgment of yourself and feelings of resentment lead to pent-up frustrations and grudges, causing an inner war because you're holding on to what happened in the past.

For example, let's say someone disrespects you, triggering your insecurities and causing you to act defensively and react emotionally. If someone strikes a nerve and brings out the worst in you, it's an alert that a false belief is limiting your progress. You only get upset and retaliate when something resonates with you; reactions reveal what you believe is lacking within yourself, thereby reaffirming a false belief of being inferior.

When you don't accept someone's disparaging remarks as truth, you remain in alignment with your Higher Self, free from fear and false beliefs, knowing that their unjust behavior stems from their own fears and insecurities. Therefore, you don't engage with their antics; instead, you remain calm, confident, and poised, which allows you to keep your dignity when challenged. The ego, which houses insecurities, is loud, whereas the Higher Self is quiet—it's an observer.

Emotional intelligence results from managing your life. This practice includes having an abundance mindset, cultivating self-awareness, and not falling prey to low vibrational energy—such as from anger, frustration, and resentment—knowing that it can create dissonance and challenging experiences. Therefore, you distance yourself from people who live in conflict, chaos, and drama.

When you are consciously aware of your behavior and your interactions with others, you become the best version of yourself because you are leading with love, being nonjudgmental, responding rather than reacting, and focusing on your goals and dreams. When you walk in the light, you live in the vibration of abundance.

But know there will be times when your emotions get the best of you. Consider physical movement or creative expression to transform your energy.

Movement and Creativity

When you are stuck in negative emotions and you can't see past what you're going through, that low vibrational energy can cause you to be unmotivated, uninterested, and unwilling to do anything. You might sit, sulk, replay what happened in the past, and ruminate over how it's making you feel. If you find yourself in the "woe is me" mindset and feel that emotional heaviness, understand that emotions are energy in motion, which means you have to take action to change the form of your energy. For instance, you can go for a walk to clear your head. You can take a fitness class to relieve stress. You can play music and dance to put yourself in a good mood.

Exercise is an act of self-love that raises your vibration. It's therapeutic, and it rejuvenates you. You can be emotionally worn out but after completing a workout feel on top of the world; that phenomenon is what runners call a "runner's high." Exercise boosts your mood because it produces endorphins, which can reduce stress and improve your well-being. It can also change your perception of a situation because as your mood changes, you see things differently.

Physical activity leads to better health, a better state of mind, and a better life. When you work out on a regular basis, you begin to see improvements in strength, weight loss, energy, mindset, etc. This practice helps to build your self-confidence and self-esteem, which strengthens your character as you learn how to become focused and disciplined. This strong sense of self and change in behavior will positively impact every area of your life.

You can also transform negative emotions into positive ones by turning your attention to a goal, dream, or hobby. When you shift your focus, you are putting your creative energy to work for you. This is how you turn pain into gain—and that's the best return on investment.

Another way of getting out of your emotions is through gratitude.

Gratitude

When we are in the midst of life's trials and tribulations, we get so wrapped up in what's going on in our heads that we tend to forget about the solution: God. We just need to recalibrate to the frequency of love, and gratitude is the best way to get there.

Gratitude is a positive state of mind that evokes happiness because you are fully present and fully aware of the generosity that God has bestowed upon you. When your attention is on God and you're thankful for everything you have and for the lessons you've learned, you are in alignment with your Higher Self because your actions are an expression of unconditional love.

Life lessons, though difficult to handle, are here to feed our soul's growth. I thank God for all of my experiences because they made me who I am today. They made me feel sad, fearful, embarrassed, ashamed, and guilty. They taught me how to adapt to change, they brought wisdom and gave me the insight to realign with my authentic self, and they shaped my character and made me stronger, more confident, and more resilient.

Ask yourself, *How do I see myself, how do I view my past, and what's my perception of the universe?* Your perception determines whether you create a victim mentality or a victor mentality. When you consider yourself abundant, the universe generous, and your past a blessing, you empower yourself to live a victorious life because you are living from an enlightened perspective.

However, when you go through challenging times, they can lead to pessimistic views that keep you from seeing the good in your life. When you are upset, do you take time to focus on what's going right in your life? Or are you solely focused on what's not working out?

The path back to the light is through gratitude, as gratitude returns the heart and mind to love. So, the next time you're feeling down, think about all the wonderful things that are going right in your life and how much you have to be thankful for.

Here's an exercise to incorporate gratitude into your daily routine.

ACTION STEP 1: Start the day by being thankful for your health, family, career, home, etc. through prayer, meditation, or journaling.

Gratitude is acknowledging what matters most in life: your relationship with God, the love of your family and friends, your health and the health of your loved ones, and being of service to others. This practice leads to fulfillment because you recognize the true value of life.

ACTION STEP 2: Before you go to bed at night, review the highlights of your day. For example: "Thank you for the wonderful visit with Mom and Dad. Thank you for helping me get my project across the finish line. Thank you for making sure I got home safely."

Gratitude is a virtue; this practice displays high moral values because you are acknowledging, appreciating, and celebrating the gifts of life. When you practice gratitude 365 days a year, you will find it to be your most rewarding habit because it builds your character and shifts your perspective, which changes your reality.

Gratitude is also the key that unlocks the door to abundance, because you're projecting your fullness into the universe, rather than expressing what's missing or what's not working out. This practice of being mindful and grateful results in an abundant future.

CHAPTER 4

MINDFULNESS AND COMMUNICATION

Because I was uncomfortable with my sexuality, I caused myself unnecessary stress and pain. I didn't want to believe it was true, so I dissociated from the real me. Ignoring my true self was my coping mechanism, but the root cause of this behavior was a lack of self-love. When you love yourself, you embody your true essence and you make changes to improve your well-being and quality of life.

Lack of self-acceptance is a heavy burden to carry because it creates mental traps that lead to distress, self-criticism, and low self-esteem. That's why we must show ourselves love, compassion, and kindness, instead of punishing ourselves. If you are struggling with self-acceptance or are experiencing something similar, ask yourself, *Would God treat me the way I'm treating myself?* God loves us unconditionally, so we should imitate his behavior.

We are all at different stages of our journey based on our self-concept and our level of awareness. To align with your Higher Self, you must change your beliefs about who you are, what you deserve, and what you are going through or have been through. Know that an abundance mindset is wholeness and brings freedom. When you recognize your worth and approve of yourself and your uniqueness, you stand in your true power, which enables you to embrace your journey, knowing that life lessons are part of your soul's evolution, as they serve your highest good.

So, what have I learned from my experience of not being my authentic self? You must stand in your truth because God is the truth. He made us who we are for a reason, and that's exactly who we need to be for our souls to be free.

When you deny your truth, you attract self-punishment because you're not soul-centered, which means you're living through the ego and projecting fear. But when you speak your truth, you embrace your authenticity, which is an expression of unconditional love. As a result, you inspire others to do the same.

I believe that in the face of adversity, we gain strength, courage, and confidence, allowing us to balance mental conflict and become vulnerable. When we open up about what we've been through, our stories can be of service to others who may be facing similar emotional experiences; vulnerability contains wisdom.

Conversely, when you don't recognize your worth or don't accept yourself for who you are, it can cause you to feel inferior and unequal due to false beliefs. The truth is, nobody is better than you, and you are not better than anyone else. We are all equal, but fear creates a division in the mind and division among us. Society conditions us to view people through labels.

While some labels can foster a sense of community, others cause separation because of our preconceptions. The ego judges or feels judged based on sexual orientation, race, ethnicity, social class, gender, etc., causing dissonance among us. That judgment stems from a fear of what we don't understand. I believe if all of humanity experienced every label placed on people, there wouldn't be separations among us; we'd become compassionate, kind, and loving toward one another, because we would have insight into how living with each of those differences would make us feel.

The truth is, our authentic state of being is unconditional love. So, let's live in that state now, rather than in fear and judgment. There's nothing stronger in the world than when we unite in love, for love is our *superpower*. It's God's frequency, which dispels the darkness.

Wouldn't it be wonderful if we *all* celebrated each other's differences? Can you imagine how different our world would be if we were mindful of our actions, were accepting, and led with love? Most likely, it would be heaven on earth—because together, we can raise the vibration of humanity through unified consciousness.

Mindfulness

Practicing mindfulness involves being cognizant of your thoughts, words, feelings, beliefs, and actions, including how you choose to respond to life's stressors. Ask yourself, *When things don't turn in my favor, will I choose to remain positive and persevere despite my circumstances, or will I succumb to fear and stay stuck in low vibrational energy?*

You can change your vibration at any time. That's the beauty of having the ability to create. But how many of us are making the most of this gift?

For instance, if you are feeling down in the dumps and looking for a mood booster, consider laughing. Your sense of humor can change your state of mind and light up a room—or even the world, for that matter. Have you ever started laughing because you heard someone else laugh? Laughter is contagious. It's a positive charge of energy that transmutes negative emotions into positive ones.

The same goes for songs. How many times have you heard a song and it made you smile, sing along, or dance? How many times has a song reminded you of a memory? How many times have you watched a movie and thought the music made the story come alive? So, why does music make you feel so good? Because it was created out of the emotion of love. The sounds and lyrics celebrate with you and comfort you, thereby changing the form of your energy.

In contrast, you can lower your vibration by watching the news, TV shows, movies, or any other content associated with violence, crime, and negativity. Those fear-based stories allow the darkness to seep in. How do you know this content is affecting you? Because it changes your mood. You start feeling fearful, anxious, scared, or depressed.

Negativity is all around us. It's in the workplace. It can be found in conversations with loved ones and friends. So it's up to us to be mindful, cultivating positivity and limiting our exposure to negativity.

What should you do when you are drawn into a negative conversation?

Number one, don't give meaning to what's being said. When you don't internalize it, it can't affect you.

Number two, steer the conversation in the right direction by changing the subject or giving the other person a genuine compliment. When you compliment someone, it changes their mood. The same applies to changing the subject; interjecting positivity can liven things up.

Number three, surround yourself with positive, like-minded people who live in high vibration and are rooted in optimism. When you elevate your circle, you elevate your life.

The same principle applies when you are going toward your goals and dreams. It's important to have supportive and caring people in your corner because there will be days when you will need emotional support—that word of encouragement or extra dose of confidence to remind you that you have what it takes to succeed. When you surround yourself with empowering people who see the best in you, want the best for you, and speak life into you, they bring out the best in you. That's why it's important to curate your inner circle.

Another helpful tip when pursuing your dreams is to identify a mentor in your field of study. When you observe and learn from people who have the career and lifestyle you seek, you soak up a lifetime of their knowledge, experience, mistakes, and wins, which sets you up for success.

But know that it's the daily actions you take to achieve your ambitions that change you inside and out, because this transformational process is how you realize your full potential and change the course of your life. Going after your dreams requires you to become independent, get your priorities straight, use your time wisely, and go the distance. Dream chasers don't travel in a pack; you have to be willing to go it alone so that you can put in the daily effort to improve yourself and apply yourself, which requires focus, discipline, and self-regulation.

Working toward your dream is an invisible battle between your heart and mind, as this journey is either you *for* you or you *against* you; you have to be willing to work for a long period of time before you see the fruits of your labor. You also have to be self-aware so you can shift your perspective to push past perceived limitations when faced with challenges. Otherwise, you'll spiral out of control when things don't go your way.

Some people believe that dreams are far-fetched, unrealistic, and unattainable, while others throw caution to the wind and jump right in with both feet to attain them. What separates these two groups? Beliefs. Beliefs set you up to rise or fall, to live out your dream or succumb to fear-based thinking. God would never have put a dream in your heart if you weren't meant to achieve it.

That's why it's important to stay tuned to God's frequency of faith, trust, and belief so that you don't fall into the trap of self-pity. You must know it's through risk, mistakes, and struggle that you become stronger, wiser, and more resilient. As a result, you'll no longer be the person others knew in the past. Why? When you prioritize yourself, your mindset and behavior change, which, in turn, changes your reality. With focus, discipline, dedication, and a relentless drive to achieve, you ignite an inner fire that cannot be extinguished.

That's what dreams are for: they allow you to reach your true potential, showcase your greatness, and inspire others to do the same. So dreams shouldn't be filed away in the mind as *maybe*, or *I can't*, or *someday I will*. They should be front and center in the conscious and subconscious mind—processed, lived, and realized.

Still, some people hesitate to go after their dreams because they measure their lives by a number and believe their best years are behind them. But this is so far from the truth. It's never too late to start. Your imagination doesn't have an age limit. If you feel you've lost your zest for life, you can restore your vitality by reigniting your passion. When you focus on the things that excite you and bring you fulfillment, you make your life meaningful.

The truth is, age is just a number. You can change your life at any time. Each day that you wake up is yet another opportunity you've been blessed with to create the life you desire. So, with all the same wonder, enthusiasm, and playfulness you had as a child, be ready, willing, and eager to take on the day. When you are curious, interested, adventurous, and focused, you live life to the fullest. Remember, your future is merely a reflection of what you are doing *right now*.

It's also important to be stubbornly optimistic and speak life into yourself with positive words.

Word Choice

The words that direct your life begin in your mind. Your inner voice has a frequency; the thoughts you're thinking and the emotions associated with those thoughts can create faith and belief or fear and disbelief. Your critical inner voice will take you down a rabbit hole if you let it.

Where does that voice come from? Your self-limiting thoughts—the impostors who try to steal your joy. These impostors play with your heart and mind. They show up when you are trying something outside of your wheelhouse, making you question yourself and your abilities. They will tell you that you are not as good as you think you are.

Who sends these self-limiting thoughts? Your paradigm, of course, which I like to call tomfoolery. Your paradigm tries to fool you by saying, "Wait a minute. Where do you think you're going? You can't do that! You've never done this before."

That critical inner voice also leads to assuming the worst-case scenario will come to pass, which is irrational thinking. How many times have you created a scenario in your head because you made an assumption? When you assume things instead of asking questions and seeking the facts, you create illusions and misunderstandings. You jump to conclusions because you don't have hard evidence at hand. If you don't have the facts, you shouldn't make assumptions, because they promote negative thinking and are a misuse of consciousness.

When you are aware of your critical inner voice, you will dismiss unhealthy dialogue and tell the impostors that they were not invited. You will reprogram your subconscious mind to work for you, which will give you the self-confidence needed to forge ahead. You will also seek the truth and facts, rather than assumptions, knowing communication is a two-way street.

Our voice is a gift from God, and our words can lift us up or bring us down. Consider how many times you have heard the word "hate" used in a conversation like it's no big deal—"I hate this" or "I hate that." "Hate" is a strong word with negative connotations, and it should be removed from our vocabulary, along with "shut up," "duh," "stupid," "dumb," "ugly," "I can't," and "I am not."

How many times have you heard people say, "I'm feeling down"? What about "I am tired," "I'm feeling lazy," or "I can't wait until the weekend"? Here's another one: "When I retire, I can't imagine being home with him or her all day—it would drive me crazy." Why on earth would you want to set your-self up to receive negative experiences? Words are energy, and the energy you emit returns to you. You can't go through life speaking negativity and expect to have positive results; you can't speak lack and expect abundance. To live abundantly, you must choose words that represent your Higher Self, words that express gratitude, love, and integrity.

As we've discussed, words are very powerful because they convey what you believe—and what you believe, you receive. You can speak the life you desire into existence, as long as you believe what you're saying, adopt the feeling that it already exists, and then follow up with action. For example: "Thank you, God, for the overflow of abundance that I am now expe-riencing in all areas of my life."

It's up to us to draw into our lives what we would like to receive by using words like "thank you" and "I am." The words "thank you" describe what you already have, and the words "I am" identify and affirm who you are. In the Bible, God is referred to as "I am," so when you say, "I am," you are acting as one with God. You are acknowledging God at work within your words.

For example, you could say, "I am limitless, and I achieve whatever I set my mind to. I am whole in mind, body, and spirit. I am blessed and highly favored today, tomorrow, and for eternity."

Now consider how many times you've heard people say, "I want." When you want something, you create resistance due to a scarcity mindset. Instead, say, "I have" or "I am grate-ful for," which are expressions of existence and abundance. Positive affirmations and positive self-talk state who you are;

when you identify with what you're saying, it becomes your reality.

Your words can also influence and change someone else's energy. What you say and do can make someone smile, or it can make them cry. Ask yourself, *What is my motive, the emotion, behind what I'm about to say?* There is always a motivating factor behind our words and actions—is it love, encouragement, compassion, empathy, jealousy, anger, revenge, greed, lust, envy, or control? Then, ask yourself, *What is my intention? Is it to get a point across, is it to prove that I'm right, is it to bring the other person up, or is it to bring them down?*

The words you choose come from your heart and reveal your character, so the best course of action comes from showing love, compassion, and kindness—and using words to bless, motivate, and encourage others. Of course, there are times when this is easier said than done. How many times have you disagreed with someone, leading to a back-and-forth fight with hurtful words? How many times have you thought to yourself, *Why did I say that?* When the heart isn't vibrating in love, words become impure. They are like stingers, and the other party feels the pain they cause.

If you disagree with someone, you can still get your point across respectfully by being thoughtful with your words, and not raising your voice or trying to chip away at their self-esteem. When hurtful words do escape the mouth, you can't take them back, but you can ask for forgiveness. When you forgive yourself and the other party, you release the anger and resentment that you're holding on to; you make peace in your heart, which returns you to a state of wholeness because your actions are motivated by grace and unconditional love.

Now let's think about how many times we've engaged in gossip. It doesn't make us feel good, right? When we gossip, we are focusing on other people's business over our own; we are judging, which reveals our shortcomings, not theirs. It's also a waste of our precious time and energy. Why would we take time out of our day to criticize, envy, or betray the confidence of someone? Those behaviors come from the ego, the lower self, which is a big bully that tries to make itself appear superior by pointing fingers at others. But in actuality, the ego feels threatened and insecure.

When you speak from your Higher Self, you speak from the heart, and you're mindful of the words you choose, knowing they have the power to create blessings in your life and the lives of others. You also understand that you can transform your life through the power of prayer and meditation.

Prayer and Meditation

How many of us wake up in the morning and immediately reach for our phones? We check emails and social media but bypass the most important communication of all, with God.

When you put God first, you set yourself up for a successful day. This daily act of communing with him and trusting him sustains you. As you nourish your relationship with God, he shows up for you by providing grace, support, and strength, which becomes visible to the world through your daily actions.

Prayer can be a conversation, an expression of gratitude, or an opportunity to request guidance, protection, divine intervention, and answered prayers. This sacred practice also allows you to turn your burdens over to God, which releases resistance and brings inner peace.

Matthew 21:22 (KJV), states, "And all things, whatsoever ye shall ask in prayer, believing, ye shall receive." This teaching of Jesus is crystal clear: *you must believe.* What's the definition of belief? The certainty that something exists. Therefore, you have to believe that you've already received what you're asking for in prayer. Remember, belief is threefold: the mind, emotions, and divine will working in harmony. Your energy radiates belief when you thank God in advance with heart-felt emotion for fulfilling your request, which is an act of thanksgiving because your vibration is filled with gratitude, contentment, and fulfillment. Those feelings give your prayer life. Lastly, you must demonstrate your belief through your unwavering actions.

Meditation is another way to connect with God because you are elevating to higher consciousness by quieting the mind and tapping into your intuition, the all-knowing frequency. Meditation is a vehicle of manifestation, as it energetically aligns you with your goals, dreams, and aspirations. It also develops and strengthens your intuition, improves your ability to focus, sparks your creativity, provides awareness, benefits your well-being, and deepens your faith. It's the art of honoring your inner knowing and acknowledging your completeness.

Meditation doesn't have to be a time-consuming event. You can practice it for ten to fifteen minutes each day. I've found that the best time to meditate is in the early morning hours before everyone else is awake—no phones ringing, no emails or text messages. The early morning allows for uninterrupted one-on-one time with God.

There are many types of meditation that you can practice. You just need to determine the one that is best for you. For example, I enjoy mindfulness meditations, which involve structuring my day by describing what I am going to accomplish. This practice guides the subconscious by impressing instructions upon it. When you set an intention, you become the designer of your life; you set the vibration, which then becomes the tone of the day.

Ultimately, mindfulness meditation is about training the mind to focus on thoughts, ideas, and visions that elevate you and your life. This brings us to the next chapter, the importance of focus and action.

CHAPTER 5

FOCUS AND ACT

Why didn't I write this book sooner? I was still learning my most valuable life lesson: self-love—realizing my worth. Knowing your worth is the holy grail of personal development because you can only rise in life as high as you believe you can.

If you feel unworthy, you will put limits on yourself, which can cause you to talk yourself out of doing the things you want to do. You will begin to create negative scenarios, asking yourself questions like *What if I fail?* or *What if what I create is not well-received?* Once again, this dynamic is your paradigm working behind the scenes to thwart your will.

Let's face it: the paradigm is a broken record repeating the same old worn-out pattern of behavior because it's based on your self-concept—who you believe you are and what you believe you deserve. So, if you are trying something you haven't done before and you don't know your worth, that false belief of inferiority can cause you to feel unsure of yourself. As a result, you will begin to question yourself and your abilities, which creates a feeling of unease; this change in mood then prevents you from taking action, thus keeping you in your comfort zone. What is the comfort zone? It's where you feel safe and secure, preferring what you know over what you don't know, because you don't want to immerse yourself in something that feels uncomfortable.

Let's think about this for a minute: we are afraid to move forward in life because of our feelings. Our feelings are the roadblock to abundance; a lack of progression in life is the result of identifying with *not feeling worthy*. This sounds foolish, right? Once again, our feelings are felt in the body; they are the result of what we think and believe. It's that physical feeling that overwhelms us and stops us from taking action. With this awareness, you can change your mindset and shift your vibration, knowing that discomfort leads to improvement.

So, ask yourself, *Is what I'm currently doing an expression of my true potential, or am I staying where I don't have to challenge myself.* When you get out of your comfort zone, you become the best version of you. The bottom line is we are not meant to sit in the stands, idolizing the ones who've made it. We were designed to be on the field having fun, learning, playing the game, and being of service to others.

I get it—everyone loves to feel at ease in a familiar place, but that comfort doesn't get you where you want to go in life. You must tell yourself that where you are going is going to be so much more rewarding than where you've been. The uneasiness you go through as you take steps toward your dream strengthens your character, and it allows you to perfect your craft.

The discomfort of change is how you elevate. You can't get to the top of a mountain and enjoy the beautiful views without first climbing it. The daily, cumulative effort you put in conditions you for success. Discipline, focus, and consistency create a steady rhythm that builds structure, which brings you into harmony with what you desire.

So, why do we play it safe? Because big dreams can be intimidating. They require courage, resilience, patience, focus, and fearlessness. They ask you to believe in yourself and step into the unknown.

But it's important to remember you were born to create. That being said, what is there to be afraid of? The only limits in life are the ones you place on yourself.

In short, if you want to follow your dreams, you must focus and take action.

Focus

There are two ways to live life. One is to go through the motions on autopilot, and the other is to be fully present, creating the life you desire through your focused efforts. When you look back on your life, which one will you be most proud of?

It wasn't until I started writing this book that I fully understood the importance of focus. Focus is a medium of exchange; your time and attention are the instruments that acquire what you desire. When you're focused, you are transferring your divine energy to create your desired outcome, and when the time is right, the culmination of your concentrated energy takes on physical form in your reality. Focus is a life-changing tool. When applied properly, the act of focusing is your currency, and it creates better habits, a better lifestyle, and a better you.

According to the Wealth Research Group, only 2 percent of people fulfill their dreams.[3] That's a shockingly low percentage! What's keeping people from making their dreams a reality? I believe it's a lack of focus.

There are 1,440 minutes in each day, and what you spend your time focusing on affects every aspect of your life: health, family, relationships, career, fitness, and finances. We often don't realize how much time we spend focusing on things that are unproductive, negative, or out of our control—for example, worrying about what happened in the past or what could take place in the future, work problems, family drama, the news, texts, social media, television, etc. What you spend your time focusing on, you create more of in your life. If you focus on a problem, you make it bigger. If you focus on a solution, you create your desired outcome. When you focus on other people's business, it's unproductive and can lead to judgment, envy, jealousy, and wasted time.

Ask yourself, *How am I using my creative power—my focused energy—to change my life for the better?* You have the choice to focus on what you want or what you don't want, whether you'll work toward your desired life or spend your downtime watching TV. Many things may capture your attention, but manifesting what you truly desire requires laser focus.

Print out the following question and post it in every room in your home until you become consciously aware of it: *What am I focusing on?* Your focused efforts can change your self-concept, your health, and your fitness habits, creating the lifestyle you desire and taking you places you've never been before. When you see the value of focus, your life will change

---

3   Lior Gantz, "Why 98% of People Die without Fulfilling Their Dreams," Wealth Research Group, July 17, 2016, https://www.wealthresearchgroup.com/why-98-of-people-die-without-fulfilling-their-dreams/.

forever because you will be aware of and in control of your creative power.

It's also important to know that you can only maximize your productivity by focusing on one thing at a time. Focusing on multiple things just scatters your efforts in different directions, leaving unfinished projects.

When you fall in love with what you're doing, you become hyperfocused on creating the results you desire, completely absorbed in the task. That concentrated energy holds power because your heart, mind, and divine will are in alignment to manifest your desired outcome.

We all have dreams we'd like to pursue, but what's keeping us from acting on them? Most of the time, it's because of fear and feeling unworthy. At other times, it's because of distractions and a lack of self-discipline.

That's why self-awareness is so important; you have to be cognizant of what you are spending your time and energy on. When you focus on the things that are going to turn your life around, your life gets better.

What type of person must you become to bring your dreams to life? Someone whose mindset mirrors their actions. A person who believes in what they are doing never gives up and isn't afraid to start at the bottom and work their way up. Think of all the billion-dollar companies that started in a garage. Those entrepreneurs had an idea, created a vision, gave it their attention, and brought it to life. It doesn't matter how big the dream is; if you can think it, see it, feel it, believe it, and focus on making it happen, it will happen.

It's also important to remember that you cannot let others' opinions distract you. Suppose you tell someone what you are going to do, and they say to you, "Do you think you can do that? Do you think that's a good idea?" You need to see their reaction for what it is: fearful words generated from a false belief. When you don't give meaning to what's being said, you don't allow others' opinions to affect you. People don't create your life—you do. Keep focusing on what matters most to you, act without regard for fearful words, and never look back.

As we've discussed, big dreams often require you to go into hermit mode and fly solo. Why? Because mindful separation creates elevation. When you take time to identify and release the things that are holding you back, you can shift your focus toward creating daily practices that align with your vision. Consequently, your desired reality will come to pass because you've changed your standards and habits.

Conversely, if you stay in your comfort zone or allow distractions and interruptions to cause you to lose focus, your desires will remain out of reach. Therefore, you have to focus on what will propel you forward, because *the act of focusing is the law of attraction.*

Act

When you admire successful people, what do you applaud? Their mindset. They know who they are, which means they have a strong sense of self. Consequently, they don't allow their emotions or critical inner voice to stop them from taking action, which means they are willing to take risks and overcome obstacles.

That's the key to achieving your dreams: you must know your worth, your thoughts and emotions must remain positive, and you must make a decision to act. Every day brings new events, and there will be highs and lows; your behavior will determine what your journey is like.

Picture the earth rotating. There's no resistance; it doesn't stop and think about whether it wants to continue to rotate. It harmoniously plays by the rules of the universe. When you mirror nature's nonresistant state and embrace change and challenges, you remain in harmony.

In contrast, when you let your emotions get the best of you, you create disharmony and resistance. That's why self-awareness and emotional intelligence are so important: you must be able to self-correct. It's through self-belief, self-regulation, and the use of your critical thinking skills that you can solve problems, overcome obstacles, and achieve positive results.

The five main reasons why people don't act and, therefore, don't achieve their goals in life are a lack of belief in oneself, fear, procrastination, distractions, and excuses. You need to coach yourself through each of these self-imposed obstacles.

First, if you don't believe in yourself, who will? Believing in yourself is the only way to succeed. There will be days when you wake up and say, "Can I really do this?" But doubt is short-lived when you believe in yourself and in what you are doing. Believing is knowing that you have everything you need to achieve your goals because the power within you is far greater than any obstacle you will ever face.

Second, fear tries to mess with your mind. Sometimes, your dream is so big that it frightens you. You worry because you don't know everything you need to know and how to do it. Dreams require you to study, learn new skills, make mistakes, and find solutions—and the universe is here to support you. When you ask a question, the answer will come to you through a thought, a family member, a friend, an article, a book, or another avenue.

Third, we procrastinate and avoid the things we need to get done, because we feel unmotivated due to a negative mindset.

Where does this behavior get us? The same place as the other time stealers and time wasters—nowhere. No one can make you do anything. If you desire change, you must become the change you'd like to see by developing a positive attitude and taking action. You can motivate yourself to make a change by imagining how your life would be if you *didn't* change.

Fourth, distractions prevent us from achieving our goals because they capture our attention. Why does this happen? A lack of self-discipline. That's why there are "the haves and the have-nots"; disciplined people create the life they desire, and the undisciplined don't. You must be willing to block out all distractions and remain focused, because everything you want in life is waiting for you on the other side of discipline. Discipline allows you to see what you are truly capable of, and that is *greatness*.

Fifth, we come up with excuses as to why we put things off. We've all done it; we come up with a million reasons why we can't get started, like "I don't have time," "I can't take that risk," or "I'm too old." Where do these self-defeating thoughts get you? Nowhere. They're a waste of time. Year after year goes by and nothing changes. Excuses prevent you from creating the life you desire, because they are rooted in false beliefs.

Now, take a moment to think about what these five mental barriers have in common. *They are all trying to steal your attention to prevent you from fulfilling your desires.* To change your life, you must take action to overcome these self-imposed obstacles. Pursuing your dreams requires a higher level of commitment. You must be willing to work on them every day and give them your full attention. Yes, it will require a strong work ethic, and at times it won't be easy. But know that when you do what you love, you are on point as a co-creator, and that's exactly what God created us to do: birth our desires.

We all have God-given gifts, talents, and strengths; you just need to determine what yours are and then become an expert in those areas. You must be willing to invest in yourself by mastering your craft, finding a mentor, and doing research to learn everything you can about your field of study. We all can turn our passions into a paycheck, so don't live with the regret of not seeing your dreams come to pass. Instead, spend time focusing on the things that liberate you, enrich you, and move you forward. You come alive when you step outside of your comfort zone—that's when you are truly living.

That's why choosing an occupation shouldn't be based on salary; it should be based on going after the things that capture your heart. When you create from the heart, you feel alive, excited, and connected to a greater purpose. The conscious creative effort you put forth has the power to produce extraordinary results and create amazing opportunities.

However, you must have a compelling reason to want to change your life. Otherwise, you won't take action. That leads us to the importance of purpose, intention, and motive.

ACTION STEP 1: Unlock your purpose.

I believe the soul is drawn to things that it's curious about or desires to express out of pure love. When you focus on the things that grab your attention, spark your interest, or you can't get enough of, it's like falling in love; there's an undeniable passion.

When you have a purpose, you have a meaningful reason to take action. For example, my purpose is to be of service to others by sharing what I've learned and will continue to learn in my personal development journey.

ACTION STEP 2: Set your intention.

Intentions give meaning to your work, and they state your desired outcome. Not only do they align you with the vibration of what you desire, they also bring about what you desire because they assume belief. For example, my intention for this book is to equip future generations with intellectual, emotional, and spiritual richness—the knowledge required to create an abundant life.

ACTION STEP 3: Identify your motive.

Motives come from the heart. For example, my motive for this book is love—to be in harmony with God, each other, and our dreams and aspirations so we can live abundantly.

Once you've identified your purpose and stated your intention and motive, you can set yourself up for success by creating a thank-you script. Why do thank-you scripts work? Because a script is physical, which means your dream is already in your reality. Thank-you scripts acknowledge fulfillment.

Here is an exercise in scripting.

ACTION STEP 1: Write down your dream in the present tense, expressing gratitude as if it has already happened.

For example: "Thank you, God, that I am now doing what I love to do, renovating houses. My energy is through the roof, and I'm ready and eager to take on the day. I'm inspired and full of ideas, and I feel very fortunate.

"I love the crew that I am working with. They've become like family to me, and we enjoy working together. We show up with smiles on our faces; we laugh, joke, and genuinely care about each other, and we take pride in our work. Together, we have renovated an endless number of beautiful homes for so many wonderful families, and we are taking on more and more projects as we speak. With the additional work, we are now adding more crew members.

"The fulfillment and financial rewards that I am receiving are far beyond my wildest dreams. I feel like a magnet to abundance. Now, I'm showing my appreciation by starting a charity to build homes for the homeless.

"Just wanted to thank you again, God. My heart is filled with love and gratitude for your generosity."

ACTION STEP 2: Read the script every day for ninety days, and form a mental image of yourself living your dream life. Don't forget to infuse your words with love as you read it.

ACTION STEP 3: Play the role of the person you described in the script by adopting the qualities, habits, and skills required.

In addition to a thank-you script, you can also create a vision board—a collage of images, objects, and affirmations—to help manifest what you desire. For instance, it could be a picture of a house you'd like to attract. It could be a book cover that you create before writing the book. It could be an affirmation that you write down to empower yourself.

Visual representations of your goals and dreams get the "wheel of fortune" turning in your favor, because you are focusing your energy on your desires and making them a part of your physical reality. However, these tools are only effective when followed up with inspired action, which is passion, focus, belief, and commitment in motion. Action is required to bring dreams to life.

That's why self-awareness is so important—your current job, relationship, fitness habits, and financial status are all based on what you've focused on and acted on in the past. They reveal to you how you've managed your life thus far, and they are a reflection of your self-concept.

So, to become the change you'd like to see, you have to adopt a fearless and focused mindset and apply yourself. But it all starts with understanding what ignites you.

We all have dreams and aspirations. Ask yourself, *What lights me up? What do I believe in? What am I drawn to? What stirs my creativity? What did I enjoy doing when I was a child? What am I naturally good at? What do I like to study? What can I do that will make a positive impact in the world and help others?* Our passions lie in our emotions; that's why it's important to do what you love.

You have everything you need to create the life you desire, but action is required. So make it your mission to be a part of the 2 percent club. Together, we can increase that number, for God's sake and ours! That being said, don't just live *with* your dream; instead, start *living* your dream today because it's an act of self-love.

CHAPTER 6

SELF-LOVE

For most of my life, I cared way too much about what other people thought of me. My insecurities made me feel inadequate. At times, I didn't stand up for myself and I could be easily swayed by others. As a people pleaser, I put others' needs before my own.

What's the cause of this behavior? Living in fear-based energy due to a false belief of being inferior, which is not recognizing your worth. As we've discussed, false beliefs create learned behaviors, such as negative self-talk and self-criticism, which block the recognition of love. Consequently, you will receive experiences to wake you up to your worth, to show you just how valuable you are. It's through the difficult times—heartbreak, rejection, unrequited love, betrayal, etc.—that you learn to love and value yourself. When you recognize your worth, you identify with love and come into union with your Higher Self, which lights you up from the inside out, showcasing just how abundant you are.

That's why it's important to do the inner work, so you can identify the core issues that need to be addressed. Ask yourself, *How did my experiences from childhood and later in life shape me?* When you reflect on your fears and insecurities, you can identify the false beliefs that are preventing you from being your best self. You also come to understand how the people on your path help you to overcome those false beliefs.

Self-Realization

In Chapter 1, we discussed how false beliefs are typically the result of stressful childhood events, such as divorce, financial problems, and illness, among others. Major life stressors cause mental and emotional chaos, which creates a distraction for the family unit, causing the focus to turn toward remedying or healing from the adverse situation the family is facing. If you observe this behavior as a child, your perception will likely be that what's happening outside yourself is the main priority, because that's where the focus lies: on the problems, disappointments, or grief. Therefore, you unknowingly create a false belief that what's happening outside yourself is more important than your own needs, thereby causing you not to recognize your worth.

For example, maybe your family struggled to make ends meet while you were growing up. This experience can cause you to feel inferior to others because you perceive people who have money and material possessions as being better than you, thereby leading you to believe your worth lies in the outside world. Consequently, as an adult, you may be ambitious and strive to become successful, while still being unaware that you're tying your worth to things outside yourself. In this state of mind, your identity is one of fear and surviving, instead of love and thriving.

When you believe your worth lies outside of you, you will strive to prove your worth in your relationships and career, and you will care about others' opinions because you don't feel good enough. What happens if a relationship ends, or you lose your job? You will likely feel empty and unstable because you don't know who you are without those people or things. When you have a deflated self-concept, you're not living in a state of love and wholeness.

Self-awareness is needed to recognize a lack of self-love; otherwise, the universe will continue to provide you with experiences that show you who you are based on your projected fears and insecurities. For example, if you don't reveal your authentic self, you will attract people who conceal aspects of their identity. Or, you will attract people who bring up a topic of discussion that highlights what you have suppressed, are running away from, and are unwilling to address.

Another sign of a lack of self-love is when you become suspicious of a person who is showing you love. You begin to think they are being too nice or that they have a hidden agenda. Why? Because you haven't identified with love for self, so you resist it. You attract who you are. Consequently, you will feel more comfortable in relationships with emotional distance. To identify with love, you must know your worth, because love is wholeness.

When you lack self-love, you don't prioritize yourself, and as a result, you attract experiences in which people show you through their words and actions that you're not a priority for them. You may also be easily influenced and led by others, or you may feel the need to please people and put them first. When you value the needs of others over your own, you abandon yourself. Simply put, you give everyone your best, except for you.

It's very important in life to help, support, and care for others, but not at the expense of your well-being. Consider: *Will this make me happy, or am I doing it out of obligation or to please someone else?* You must be able to say no to others and not feel guilty about it.

When you do what people want you to do but your heart's not in it, you are ignoring your own needs. When your primary focus is on making others happy instead of yourself, you deny your happiness. When you look to others to make decisions for you, you lose sight of your divinity.

It's helpful to seek guidance and counsel from others to gain different perspectives, but ultimately, you are the only one who knows what's right for you. When you lead from your Higher Self, you start thinking about what pleases you and you use your higher mental faculties—reason, intuition, memory, and perception—to help you make informed decisions.

Imagine God saying, "My dear heart, I love you unconditionally and I want the best for you, but you have to want the best for yourself. I gave you free will to decide. Awaken to and embody the love that lies within you. Embrace your abilities, and stand in your fullness."

Self-love is seeing yourself as God sees you: complete in his fullness. When you hold yourself in high regard, you become the center of your universe, not someone else's. You also come to understand that your time and energy are valuable and should be used to focus on your personal growth.

Self-love is setting high standards that show the world how much you love and value yourself. Look at every area of your life and ask yourself, *What are my current standards for my relationship, career, health, and finances?* If you have low standards, you may accept things as they are and limit yourself by not taking action. But when you have high standards, you live an intentional life where you are consciously aware of your goals, habits, and behavior. You take action, knowing you are in control of your destiny.

So, if you want to change your life, you must be willing to reinvent yourself. First, take a moment to reflect on your lifestyle, as this is your progress report, showing you how you've acted in the past. It puts a spotlight on what you have manifested through your focused efforts. It reveals your past mindset and behaviors that have formed your current standards, habits, and routines. Next, look around to see if your environment is conducive to growth. Then ask yourself, *Is what I'm currently doing every day pushing me forward or holding me back?* You must become the person you desire to be.

For example, if you'd like to attract a loving partnership, adopt the qualities that you admire in the type of person you are seeking. Like attracts like; the qualities you admire in others are a reflection of yourself. They are in your consciousness and brought to your attention because your soul longs to expand and express your true self. You just have to activate those aspects of yourself by recognizing those qualities as *you* and then taking action to prove that they are real. You must become the love of your life before the love of your life can arrive.

That's why it's important to study yourself, so you can identify areas of improvement. When you understand that you are the only one who is minding the store, you will take responsibility for what you are experiencing in your reality and will hold yourself accountable for your feelings and actions. You will pick yourself up when you have a challenging day or when negative thoughts surface, knowing you are the primary source of your fulfillment. You will show up for yourself by taking care of your needs first.

Self-respect says, "I matter. I love myself. I am important," which means you fill your cup up before you pour your energy into others. When you run the show, you create a healthy, balanced, and stable life. Your reality is a direct reflection of your self-concept. The actions you take to improve yourself and your life represent what you believe you deserve.

If you desire a high-quality life, you must review your daily progress, asking, *What did I do today to improve my mental and emotional state? What did I accomplish today? Did I learn a new word? Did I take time to read in order to acquire new knowledge, challenge my beliefs, and be open to different perspectives? Did I step outside my comfort zone? Did I demonstrate acts of abundance?*

The goal is to grow each day. When you recognize your worth and accept what you've been through as part of your journey, you realize you are not broken, merely falsely conditioned based on past experiences and learned behaviors. Through self-realization, you can lighten the load and release the illusions, rather than living through them. This release, coupled with choosing whom you spend your time with, is how you reclaim your power and live an abundant life.

The People on Our Paths

In addition to knowing your worth, self-love involves evaluating the company you keep. Ask yourself, *Am I spending time with the right people?* Your social circle determines who you become because you can be easily influenced by others' behaviors, causing you to pick up on their attitudes, habits, values, vocabulary, outlook on life, etc. You can unintentionally let others lead you down the wrong path.

That's why it's important to be mindful of your inner circle: it's a reflection of you. When it comes to the people in your life, you must use the power of discernment—the act of having good judgment by honoring your intuition and listening to your heart. When you are discerning, you can see a person's true character through their behavior.

People show you who they are—not once, not twice, but many times. So, when you meet someone, it's important to ask the right questions and pay attention to their words and actions. Ask yourself, *Are they bringing me up or bringing me down? Are they kind? Do they make me a priority? Do they offer stability? Do their actions match their words? How do they treat others? Are they a good listener? Do they respect me? Do they show empathy and compassion? Are they investing in me?*

As we've discussed, the people you surround yourself with and the people who cross your path show you who you believe you are. They bring awareness to the underlying issues that you need to address within yourself. They are catalysts for healing your shadow side.

The people in your life treat you the way you unknowingly treat yourself, so when someone's actions trigger you, take a moment to reflect on why they upset you. For example, rejection is a lesson served when you are not consciously aware that you are rejecting yourself. Rejection is God's protection, teaching you to recognize your worth and identify with love for self so that you can project wholeness.

When you don't know your worth, you can hold on to an unhealthy relationship because you are dependent on that person for your emotional and mental stability, which can lead to ignoring red flags, living in conflict, feeling defeated, and making excuses for others' disrespectful behavior or transgressions.

When you accept dissonance in a relationship, your energy is of fear, not love—which leads to resistance, complacency, and tolerance of dysfunctional behavior. What's the root cause of viewing life through a victim mindset? False beliefs, such as codependency and inferiority, and being consumed by your emotions. This false narrative creates a false perception. In this state, you may create an illusion that things will get better. Perhaps they will, but you can't fall into wishful thinking; you must break through the illusions to see the truth. You must invest in people who walk their talk, meaning their actions match their words. Otherwise, you are welcoming inconsistent behavior and unstable energy into your life, as well as lowering your standards by accepting the bare minimum.

The purpose of these unhealthy relationships is to wake you up to your worth. If you have to bend to someone's will, or if you try to bend their will to do right by you, ask yourself, *Is this the right person for me?* You can't change anyone, and they can't change you. You can only change yourself.

When you make relationship decisions based on potential versus reality, you are wearing rose-colored glasses, seeing things the way you want them to be rather than the way they are. When you create illusions, it's because you expect people to think and act as you would—but they are not you. They don't have the same morals, values, and experiences you've had. Therefore, they can't see through your eyes.

When you lack self-love, you attract resistant relationships in which both parties trigger each other's insecurities so that both can awaken to their shadow sides. Enduring rejection or betrayal, feeling unappreciated and unloved, or not having your needs met are all mirrors showing you that you don't know your worth. The lessons keep coming until one day you gain awareness, which wakes you up. That's when you say, "Okay, okay, I get it. I get it. Finally! I've got it! I've had enough!" This is when you put on your big-girl or big-boy pants and boss up. This is when you recognize your worth, step into your power, and take control of your life because you've awakened to your Higher Self. This is your lightbulb moment, and from this day forward, there is no going back because you've been enlightened. You can't unsee what you've seen, and as a result, you will no longer compromise your worth because you've *identified* with love.

This elevated state of mind allows you to release unhealthy attachments, which brings peace and harmony. A person who is for you will not engage in mental and emotional manipulation, make you feel confused about where you stand, or make you compete for their attention. A person who is for you will value your presence. They will stand by your side, be emotionally available, and feel excited to share their life with you because love is a verb; it is a display of mutual respect, friendship, devotion, attentiveness, appreciation, and affection.

Remember, people treat you the way you treat yourself. When you know your worth, you choose to love yourself, which means you set healthy boundaries in your relationships to meet your needs and standards because you know you deserve the best. As a result, you attract healthy, loving, balanced, reciprocal relationships that are nonresistant. Both parties work as a team, inspire and uplift one another, and challenge each other to grow. Both parties know how to love because they love themselves first.

So, don't lose yourself in someone else or settle for less than you deserve—these acts only lead to sacrificing your happiness. Instead, recognize your worth so that you can step into your fullness and become the person God designed you to be: self-assured and self-actualized.

When you stop chasing after people and outcomes, what you are seeking comes to you. Why? Because you've released resistance, which puts you in a nonresistant state. You may not receive the exact person or opportunity you desire, but that desire will be replaced with someone or something that is a better fit for your growth and your path, as God knows what's best for you. He can see what you cannot see, and he has your best interests at heart.

The art of detachment is not resisting reality, which means not trying to coerce, change, or chase after people; not trying to control outcomes; and no longer living in a vibration of longing, neediness, wanting, or despair. It's feeling satisfied and full of life. It's allowing others to be who they are, and it's living in the flow, unbothered by what you can't control.

When you are unaffected emotionally by what's happening to you or around you, you remain in a state of peace and harmony, open to receiving. When you become nonresistant, it's an act of self-love because you understand that inner war pushes away what you are asking for. *Remember, your subconscious mind is a projection of your self-concept, what you believe, and how you feel.* You attract what you need to learn so you can gain awareness, create positive change, and grow.

Just when you think you have it all under control and have learned to love yourself, you will be tested. The negative things that people say to you will echo in your mind, or you may be triggered by something you see or hear, at which time negative thoughts will cause you to slip back into your ego.

That's when you need to be ready to rise to the occasion and say, "Nice try, but I am smarter and wiser than that. Thank you, but no thank you—I no longer live in an illusion. I live in the penthouse suite, which is my Higher Self, where I have extraordinary views because my self-worth allows me to see the truth." Then you apply your six mental faculties to make good on that promise to yourself.

CHAPTER 7

MENTAL FACULTIES

As I struggled to be my authentic self, I adopted a hopeless mindset that filled me with fear and low self-esteem, because I found it difficult to accept myself. Before I knew it, I was going through the motions on autopilot, because I couldn't see past what I was experiencing. The false narrative that I had created replayed itself in my mind, reaffirming the false belief that the challenges I faced were insurmountable. I didn't apply my mental faculties to get myself out of that dark place; rather, I felt powerless and was existing in survival mode.

When you believe that what you're going through is bigger than your ability to overcome it, you succumb to worry, sadness, grief, or anger, relinquishing your power, because you've voluntarily lowered your vibration to fear. Instead, surrender the situation to God and see the bigger picture so that you can release resistance and rise into your Higher Self—love, peace, and harmony because that's home.

Our inner world creates our reality. So why are we not going there daily to design our lives, when we know that 95 percent of the time we are on autopilot? Let's apply this knowledge by cultivating self-awareness, so we can change our reality by using our inner tools to align with our desired results.

Life is a path to enlightenment, a journey to self-discovery and self-empowerment. When you lead from your Higher Self and use your higher mental faculties for your highest good and the greater good, you're acting as the highest expression of yourself, which is the energy of ultimate fulfillment. *That* is the blueprint for abundance. With a rich mindset and the use of your higher mental faculties, you can enrich the world.

As I mentioned before, our six mental faculties are reason, imagination, memory, intuition, perception, and will. They are the forces of the mind that create our reality, but they are invisible to the naked eye, which means they are out of sight and often out of mind. Our attention tends to be on the physical world, instead of tapping into our majestic gifts that lie in the unseen.

Let's discuss these invisible gifts, which unlock the magnetic potential within us.

Reason

What is the mental faculty of reason, and how do we use it? It's the power of the mind to apprehend, analyze, rationalize, compare, think logically, and form conclusions and judgments.

But what if you are not operating from your Higher Self—will you make sound decisions? Will you think clearly? To create a high-quality life, you must be self-aware, because what you continue to think about and focus on, you attract into your reality.

By practicing self-regulation, you can align with optimistic thoughts that promote positive thinking. When you make your mind your business, you keep your thoughts focused on what you desire and deserve so that you can prosper and grow.

One study found that the average person has over six thousand thoughts per day.[4] How many of us are evaluating those thoughts? How many of us are just going along with the thoughts that pop into our heads?

Just because you think something doesn't mean you should dwell on it. If a thought is not propelling you forward, dismiss it. Negative thoughts ignite fear and create resistance because they stem from false beliefs. They are nothing more than impostors trying to disguise themselves as the truth. If you don't give them the time of day, they don't stand a chance because they can't flourish without *your attention*.

When you continue to think negative thoughts or ruminate over past disappointments, it's an act of self-sabotage, which can prevent you from receiving what you're predestined to have: abundance. Fear-based thinking keeps you stuck in the past and away from your desired future. Instead, practice forward thinking. Life gets better when you shift into consciousness and cultivate intelligent thoughts that align with progress, innovation, and transformation. Remember, what you give your undivided attention to becomes your reality.

For example, stress only exists if you think the outcome of a situation is unsatisfactory. Stress is a reaction to your environment. It can be brought on by life-changing events, such as financial and relationship issues, as well as other challenges or demands that put you under pressure. Coping with stress is

---

4   Jason Murdock, "Humans Have More than 6,000 Thoughts per Day, Psychologists Discover," *Newsweek*, July 15, 2020, https://www.newsweek.com/humans-6000-thoughts-every-day-1517963.

not easy, because you perceive the change as a threat or source of dissatisfaction, which leads to a state of distress and difficulty functioning.

Stress occurs when you are emotionally triggered by a situation, such as the loss of a job, but it is nothing more than misdirected energy due to a false belief that creates resistance and unresolved fears. Stress can be the result of not accepting the outcome of a situation, not believing things will get better, or not taking action to change what you're going through. That's why practicing self-awareness is so important: it allows you to release negative thought patterns.

When you approach an adverse situation with rational thinking, you come to understand that stress is the result of a fear-based perception. This practice allows you to see things more clearly and rise above your emotions.

Life gets better by using reason rather than resisting the reality of a situation. When you release mental and emotional conflict, you restore peace and harmony in your life. Your thoughts and feelings are the equivalent of healthy eating and exercise; both are equally important in maintaining a healthy state of being.

Your thoughts and feelings highlight what you're going through. For example, when you have self-defeating thoughts and a heavy, looming feeling in your chest, it's a signal from the universe saying, "Hey, you are off track." Your emotions give you a heads-up to self-correct so that you can move out of the negativity that threatens your system. Negative feelings are an indicator of the need to change your perspective.

These alarms are set to alert us, not silence us, but how many times do we turn off our light, sit in the darkness, and continue to wallow in sadness? How many times do we think the same repetitive thoughts that reveal more of what we don't want? How many times have we felt hopeless, anxious, or depressed? We've all been there.

Sometimes, we don't even realize we are out of alignment because we lack the awareness that we've surrendered our power. When you worry, feel doubtful, or try to control people or outcomes, you disconnect from your Higher Self and descend like a popped balloon. Why? Because fear-based energy leads to resistance and irrational thinking, which leaves you feeling powerless. Instead, use reason to identify why you are feeling so bad.

Ask yourself, *What have I been thinking about that brought me to this emotional state? Is it my thoughts, or is it something that I saw or heard?* The uncomfortable situations we go through help us learn, grow, and understand ourselves better, but it doesn't do us any good to live in a state of despair. That's why it's important to be self-aware of what you are thinking and believing so you can self-correct.

Think about the time from when you woke up this morning until now. How many thoughts did you have about the past? How many thoughts did you have about the future? How much time did you spend in the present moment? It's called "the present" because what you spend your time focusing on right now creates *future presents*: your dreams and desires.

To promote positive thinking, you must make your inner voice your cheerleader and not your critic, by replacing limiting thoughts with positive ones. The story you tell yourself creates your reality, so make sure it's an undeniable triumph! When you think good thoughts about yourself and others, you in turn protect yourself from negativity. Why? Because the energy you emit is the energy you receive. I'm not saying you will never have negative thoughts—of course, you will—but you will lessen them as you retrain the mind to focus on positive thinking.

When you make it a daily practice to direct your thoughts, you live intentionally, which allows you to set yourself up for success because you go where your thoughts go. That's why setting intentions is so powerful: your focus turns toward achieving your desired results. This mindful practice allows you to outline the things you'd like to accomplish during the day, so you can then commit them to memory, write them down, and complete them. By directing your thoughts, you can also create your mood, which is the motivating factor in determining your actions. The end goal is to make your mind work for you by using reason, so you can ascend to your Higher Self through positive thinking. Next, use your imagination, so you can continue to soar to new heights.

Imagination

The second mental faculty is imagination—your creative playground. Think back to when you were a kid. Do you remember playing the imagination game? Do you remember pretending to be different characters and creating fictional stories? There is so much value in our imagination because we are creative beings. We are here to create, so why don't we use this tool daily to envision the life we desire?

Imagination is a life-changing tool because it's where creation begins. Your imagination gives you the ability to envision an abundant life: good health, a loving partnership, the lifestyle you desire, an amazing career, an overflow of prosperity, and much more. The picture you paint in your mind can be anything you want it to be because your imagination is infinite. So, ask yourself, *What do I want my future to look like and feel like?* Then envision your desired life and live in that vibration.

The subconscious mind doesn't know the difference between real and imagined; it believes what the conscious mind tells it. Therefore, your vision, feelings, and use of your senses leave an impression upon it stating who you are. When you create a descriptive vision, use your senses, and feel that it has already happened, you are using your divine will to mentally, emotionally, and physically process the fulfillment of your desires.

Imagine if we taught our children to use this tool in their everyday lives. Using your imagination sets you up for success because you are actively creating the outcome you desire.

For example, picture this: you are sitting on the bench watching your team play when your coach walks up to you and says, "Get ready—you are up to bat next." At this moment, you begin to prepare yourself mentally. In your mind's eye, you see yourself setting up for the perfect batting stance. Your feet are aligned, and your knees are bent. You feel yourself gripping the bat as you hold it out in front of you.

As you look toward the pitcher, you see him lift his left knee and throw a fastball right down the middle. As the ball approaches, you drive into the pitch, hearing the sound of the ball and bat making prime contact. You hear the crowd begin to cheer, and your eyes follow the ball as it leaves the park. You just hit a home run!

You see a smile on your face as you run the bases. You smell the bratwursts grilling at the concession stand. And, as you cross home plate, you feel the joy within emanating—for it cannot be contained.

You set yourself up for success when your imagination, emotions, and senses process the results of your desired outcome before you apply yourself to make it happen. It's an exercise in mental time travel. Your imagination allows you to see yourself in possession of your dream, your heart allows you to feel the overwhelming feeling of it being fulfilled, and your senses allow you to make it undeniably real. When you add belief, faith, gratitude, and action to the mix, the force of your will completes the transfer of your energy into your desire, making it tangible. It's through the power of alignment that your focused energy helps you carry out your vision and complete your mission.

Conversely, you can also set yourself up for failure by falling into fear-based thinking and picturing yourself striking out and losing the game; this behavior is self-sabotage, using your imagination for all the wrong reasons. Instead, use your imagination for what God intended it to do—move you forward.

It's important to have a North Star, a focal point, to guide you and give you a purposeful direction in life. Proverbs 29:18 (KJV) states, "Where there is no vision, the people perish: but he that keepeth the law, happy is he." With this pearl of wisdom, let's indulge in our imagination daily, for what we imagine in our mind's eye is what we will one day see with our very own eyes.

Your imagination is your movie, uniquely designed by you. You have twenty-four hours a day to make your life into everything you want it to be. Through the use of mental imagery, feelings, and sensations, you get to choose what you want to do, where you want to go, how you want to live, and who you want to become. You are the star of your movie, as well as the producer and director, and you get to write the script. That being said, make it a memorable blockbuster hit so that one day you can look back on your life and say, "I used my imagination to live my life to the fullest!"

Memory

The third mental faculty is memory, which stores our experiences and all of the information we've learned and acquired over the years.

Our soul—which contains our memory reel—is the only thing we can take with us when we go. So, are you going to pack a light carry-on or are you going to check your luggage? The good news is God doesn't charge those hefty baggage fees; you can bring as many loving memories with you as you'd like.

I don't know about you, but I am arriving with a caravan of moving trucks. I'm going to have a "wide load" sticker slapped on the back. I'm going to buzz the intercom at the pearly gates and say, "Saint Peter, I'm going to need a little help out here because there's a lot of love coming through!"

It's the loving memories that we'll treasure most. The magical moments that made our hearts sing. The holidays, celebrations, and little things in everyday life. The smile on someone's face when you made them feel good. The times you laughed so hard, you cried. The playful times when you were lighthearted, carefree, and fully enjoying life. These are the times worth remembering. So, let's create as many joy-filled moments as we can, because today is a gift that we can only relive in our memory.

Memory also acts as a history class, so we don't repeat the past. It highlights the mistakes we've made—the lessons we've learned—and how they made us feel. We can recall those memories to help us in the present moment when we are trying to gain a deeper understanding of something, so we can make better choices and decisions moving forward.

Another way we can use memory to our advantage is by putting it to use in our everyday lives. Scientific evidence clearly illustrates close ties between episodic memory, imagination, and predicting the future.[5] What is episodic memory? It's the ability to recollect the details of an event and the emotions associated with that event. That being said, you can shape your future reality by consciously putting detailed visions into memory. When you design your vision, engage your senses, and assume the feeling of your desired outcome, you are imprinting the experience into your subconscious mind. You are planning a future event and how you want it to play out.

For instance, if you have an upcoming work meeting, use your imagination to create a positive outcome by imagining how the meeting will take place. See yourself in a leadership role, commanding the room. Put to memory what you will say so that your speech is flawless. See yourself smiling and being charismatic and passionate about what you are presenting. Visualize everyone in the room being impressed and saying, "Wow, what a great meeting!" Next, consider what you're wearing. Plan the experience down to the mood you are in as you enter the room. Be very specific.

Now, think about the difference between the scenario I just described and scheduling a meeting on your calendar. It's like night and day. Simply calendaring an event involves no vision, feelings, use of senses, will, or memorization—and there's no desired outcome. It's just a reminder for a future

---

5   Sinéad L. Mullally and Eleanor A. Maguire, "Memory, Imagination, and Predicting the Future: A Common Brain Mechanism?," *The Neuroscientist* 20, no. 3 (June 2014): 220–234, https://doi.org/10.1177/1073858413495091.

event. But when you imagine every detail and become emotionally invested in the experience, you are using your divine will to bring it to life by describing what the vision looks like, how it makes you feel, and how it affects those around you. You are consciously storing the details and emotions in your memory to play out in the future.

Now, these are the types of memories that are worth creating because they lead to the results you desire. So, let's commit to putting them to memory while using our intuition to assist us in life.

Intuition

The fourth mental faculty is intuition, which is God's frequency being made available to us so that we can see what he sees: the truth. Your intuition is your direct line of communication with the divine realm. It's when your thoughts, feelings, and gut instincts align to get your attention. Your intuition doesn't come from thinking; instead, it's an immediate download of information.

Your intuition is all-knowing, giving you pristine clarity so you can pick up on others' intentions and motives and tell right from wrong. It issues warning signs to protect you from harm and provides ideas, solutions, and answers to your questions.

Sometimes, your intuition will stop you in your tracks so that you can become consciously aware of your surroundings. Other times, you will receive intuitive nudges, making you aware of certain behaviors, people, or situations that are not serving your highest good. Either way, when you listen to your inner wisdom and follow its lead, you will be divinely guided on the right path.

How many times have you been driving when something has told you to take a different route? How many times have you been talking to someone and sensed something was off? How many times have you felt uneasy about a choice that you were about to make or an upcoming event you were going to attend? How many times have you thought about someone and then unexpectedly you hear from them or run into them?

Your intuition empowers you by giving you an enlightened perspective. But if you are not practicing self-awareness, you may brush off these intuitive messages.

How many of us ask a computer-generated voice what the weather is like, who won a game, or to play a song? We do this, but often we don't ask our intuition to assist us in life. World leaders, visionaries, artists, poets, writers, musicians, and mathematicians, among others, obtain their ideas, guidance, and inspiration from their intuitive minds.

We have access to the most reliable and accurate internal navigation system known to humankind. It also includes a database of all the infinite knowledge and wisdom of the universe, and it's readily available for use 24/7. So let's use our God-given guidance system in combination with a healthy perspective to walk through life confidently.

Perception

The fifth mental faculty is perception, the lens through which we see life. Perception is how we interpret and process something based on our beliefs.

What is the first thing you do when you encounter an unexpected event? You immediately start to process what's being presented to you. How do you see it? How does it make you feel? How does it align with your beliefs? Just because you perceive something a certain way doesn't mean it's the truth; it may seem like the truth to you, but your perception can be skewed due to a false belief.

Remember the childhood toy, back in the day, where we would insert slides to view pictures? It's the same with life. Our beliefs created in childhood or later in life are inserted into the fabric of our being; in turn, they create our perceived reality. This is problematic when false beliefs—such as "I can't do it," "I am not ready," or "Others are better than me"—create negative self-perceptions that keep us from taking action.

Take a moment to think about how important your perception is because it's *your reality*. For example, you could be standing in line next to a stranger at a coffee shop. Your outlook on life may be brimming with optimism and endless opportunities, while the other person can't see past what's missing in their life. That's why it's important to question your perception by being aware of what you're thinking and believing.

When you become self-aware, perception is an invaluable tool because you can change your reality by changing your perception of it. For example, if you believe that a certain situation you are facing is undesirable, then this belief will become your reality. But if you view difficult times as learning experiences, you can keep your vibration high by viewing life through a lens of optimism.

Each one of us has a unique frame of reference. For example, let's say your boss calls an impromptu meeting and doesn't tell you what it's about. Why do you think he called the meeting? Are you getting a promotion? Did you do something wrong? Is your boss leaving? Are they selling the company? Are you being laid off?

By using your higher mental faculties, you can make sense of the matter. First, use memory to recollect the last time he called a last-minute meeting. What happened during that meeting? For example, he received news from upper management that he was passing along. Next, use reason to form the conclusion that everything is okay. Therefore, no emotional meaning should be assigned to the event.

On the other hand, if you are fearful of an outcome, you will most likely assume the worst-case scenario. When you assume things, you assign belief without reason. That's why it's important to question your perception and use your higher mental faculties.

Here's an example of a false perception. When you go to the gym and see twenty-year-olds in perfect physical condition, you think to yourself, *Oh, that's because they are in their twenties. Their metabolism is much faster, and it's easier for them to stay in shape.* What's wrong here? A negative perception was formed due to a false belief. Nothing is off the table unless you believe it is.

You can still have a toned body, increase your metabolism, and create more muscle mass, but doing so requires focus, discipline, and action. Why do we talk ourselves out of taking action? Because it's easier to paint a different picture than to hold yourself accountable. Misperceptions can lead to a lack of commitment, so you must change your perception to match your desired outcome.

Another misconception is that people are thinking what you're thinking. *What if they think this? What if they think that?* Nobody is thinking what you are thinking. This sentence bears repeating: *nobody is thinking what you're thinking.* People are not focused on you; they are focused on themselves and what's going on in their own lives or what you're thinking of them.

When you are concerned about other people's judgments and fearful of their perception of you, you keep yourself small, because you believe your worth comes from outside approval. This false belief can influence your behavior, because you're giving meaning and value to others' opinions of you, which is a sign that you don't know your worth. The only opinion that should matter to you is your own, because the opinion you have of yourself determines how far you advance in life.

Successful people don't sit around and ponder what others are thinking about them; they're in the driver's seat, making decisions and taking action. Remember, what you focus on, you bring to life—so don't allow anyone to capture your attention and live rent-free in your head because all you're doing is creating a negative outcome. When your focus is on others' reactions, you attract judgment because you are judging yourself.

When you trust and believe in yourself, others' opinions fall by the wayside. So instead of focusing on what other people think of you, turn your attention to what God thinks of you, for the image he sees is his reflection.

What you choose to believe can either set you free or imprison you, because your perception is your reality. So when you are facing a challenging situation, ask yourself, *Is the story I'm telling myself the only way to see it?* Then ask yourself, *Would my loved ones view what I am going through in the same light?* Most likely, they would not because they wouldn't be viewing it through your beliefs and emotions. When you are facing a life-changing event or a challenging situation that is causing you pain, your thoughts and feelings often reflect dissatisfaction, disappointment, or worry, which can lead to poor judgment.

Instead, practice self-love by being open to different perspectives; when you look at a situation in more than one way, you remain open and objective. This practice allows you to see how limited thinking can keep you trapped in your emotions. When you change the narrative playing out in your mind, the way you see a situation changes, and what you're thinking about changes, which, in turn, changes your reality.

Those of us who wear glasses and contact lenses clean them daily. The inner lens requires the same care. It needs to be free of impurities, which are negative thoughts, beliefs, and emotions. When you're aligned with your Higher Self, you swap out the survival lens for an abundance lens. Then, you use your divine will to bring your dreams to life.

Will

We've all heard the saying "Where there is a will, there is a way." What is will? Will is the sixth mental faculty that works in congruence with your mind and emotions to advance your soul. When you decide to take action and your heart's in it, your will becomes the driving force to ensure you achieve your desired results.

You can use your will to manifest anything you want when you're mentally and emotionally invested and fully committed to bringing it to life. Being strong-willed requires focus, passion, discipline, commitment, and, most importantly, belief—because without belief, nothing can get off the ground. Belief gives your dreams wings to fly.

For example, we can will a penny or a beach house—they are both in equal measure. They are both objects, after all. However, your beliefs will determine which one you attract.

This reminds me of a poem by Jessie B. Rittenhouse:

MY WAGE[6]

I bargained with Life for a penny,
And Life would pay no more,
However I begged at evening
When I counted my scanty store;

For Life is a just employer,
He gives you what you ask,
But once you have set the wages,
Why, you must bear the task.

I worked for a menial's hire,
Only to learn, dismayed,
That any wage I had asked of Life,
Life would have paid.

Life gives us what we believe we are worthy of receiving, so let's believe we deserve the best because it's the absolute truth. That being said, let's manifest a luxurious oceanside beach house.

Maybe you are thinking, *How realistic is a beach house? How could I afford such a lavish home?*

Stop right there. If you can't see it and you don't believe it, you won't be able to achieve it. If you are creating reasons why you can't have it, you won't have it, because you just talked yourself out of it. Your vision, words, thoughts, feelings, beliefs, and actions must be in alignment to obtain your desired results.

What are the fundamental ingredients required to call forth a beach house? Well, first and foremost, an abundance

---

6   Jessie B. Rittenhouse, "My Wage," in *The Door of Dreams* (Cambridge: The Riverside Press, 1918), 25.

mindset is needed to create expansion. You are primed for success when you think of successful thoughts and ideas, remove false beliefs, and grow rich beliefs. These positive actions create a ripple effect because you've changed the narrative. When you feel worthy, you will adopt the qualities, habits, and skills needed to achieve the results you desire.

Next, feel as if you already own the beach house. How would you feel? Grateful, peaceful, relaxed, and very fortunate. Now, make those feelings a part of your everyday life, and release any resistance to receiving the beach house.

When you acknowledge that you already have what you are asking for, it arrives. You don't need to question it or chase after it. It will come to you at the right time. When is the right time? When you have prepared to receive it.

You must create a product or offer a service to generate income to purchase the beach house. What is your skill or talent? What do you love to do? When you love what you do and offer a product or service that people value and need, you create demand.

So, what's the plan? Are you flipping houses, writing a book, opening a hair salon, creating an app, starting a landscaping or construction business, getting into real estate, or building an e-commerce store? We all have a God-given purpose, and when you find yours, you will attract customers or employers willing to pay for your product or service.

Next, choose a photo of your ideal beach house and place it on your vision board. Come up with a name for your new house and create a personalized sign or plaque to hang on the wall when you move in. As we discussed earlier, when you make your dream physical, you give it life.

Now, here comes the fun part: imagine the day you buy your beach house, romanticizing every detail so that you stir up joy from within, including the use of senses, gratitude, and assuming the feeling of owning the beach house. As a reminder, this practice allows you to create, process, and commit the experience to memory so that it plays out in the future.

Here is an example of envisioning yourself as a soon-to-be beachfront homeowner.

As you turn off the alarm, you practically leap out of bed. You've been waiting all week to go look at your new house. Making your way through the kitchen, you smile as you grab the real estate flyer off the fridge. It's been nice to look at, but now you're making your dream home a reality. After completing your morning rituals, you grab your keys and head out the door.

As you enter the charming coastal town, you reach Ocean Drive and are mesmerized by how the sunlight glistens on the water. As you drive by the beachfront homes, you see American flags waving in the wind, striped umbrellas, chairs planted in the sand, and a sign that reads, "Relax, you're on beach time now." Then, you notice the "For Sale" sign coming into view, which fully captivates your attention.

As you turn into the drive and park, you begin to take in the stunning views. The home is absolutely breathtaking! Your eyes are immediately drawn to the colorful array of hydrangeas that line the front porch, and there are planters placed on every other step with a vibrant display of begonias and coral bells. You hear chatter coming from behind you, and as you turn around, you see a group of surfers on the street, unloading their surfboards from their vehicles.

As you turn your attention back to the house, your eyes light up, and your heart melts as you slip into the vibe of beach life. Your dreamy state is short-lived, though, as it is interrupted by the sound of a car horn. You glance over to see your real estate agent pulling into the drive next to you. You both smile, get out of your vehicles, and exchange pleasantries.

She begins to tell you about the property, but you can't help but be distracted by your senses. You can feel the wind at your back, you can smell the salty ocean air, and the sunlight is so bright that you have to raise your hands over your eyes to create shade. You begin to hear some lively banter coming from above and notice seagulls flying overhead, followed by a flock of pelicans in flight. You stop to shake the sand from your shoes, thinking, *Wow, this is the life!*

As you step onto the front porch, you begin to appreciate the beauty of the home. It has gray shake siding, white beach-style windows, a brick chimney, gas lanterns, and a front porch with columns and a daybed swing. As you enter the house, your eyes immediately meet the floor-to-ceiling windows facing the ocean: a view that cannot be described in words, only experienced in person.

Your focus then shifts to the ambience emanating from the fireplace. Not only has it captured your attention, it has also awakened your senses, leaving you lost in the blazing embers, crackling fire, and fragrant smell of firewood, and causing you to think of the memories you will soon be creating.

As you enter the chef's kitchen, you realize you're home because you can see yourself making dinner and spending time with family and friends—and oh, the holidays, how grand those times will be! Your eyes then begin to well up with emotion as you search for the perfect place for this year's Christmas tree.

As the agent continues to show you the rest of the property, your focus turns inward. As you are overwhelmed by the love in your heart, and with a deep sense of joy and gratitude, you offer a word of thanks to God. When you come back to reality, you hear the agent say, "Would you like to make an offer?"

You reply, "The offer has already been made to the *real owner*. Let's seal the deal!"

As you're leaving, you walk onto the beach and write these six words in the sand: *My heart is in this home.*

The more vivid you are in describing your vision, the more emphasis you place on emotionally processing the outcome you desire, and the more you make it physical, the more you give it life; when your mind, emotions, and divine will are in harmony, you are committing your vision to memory to play out in the future.

Lastly, continue to use your will by immersing yourself in what you are creating. Be laser-focused and disciplined because this practice is when you are firing on all cylinders and operating at full capacity, which aligns you with the magnetic field that brings forth your desires.

You can make your life into everything you desire it to be because you have access to infinite knowledge, both within and without (e.g., your intuition, books, the internet, mentors, podcasts, tutorials, school, AI, etc.). If you can see your dream in your mind's eye, feel grateful for it in your heart, direct your focused energy to build it, and be certain that it already exists, that elevated vibration and concentrated effort will materialize your desires in your physical reality. In short, by aligning with your Higher Self and using your six mental faculties, you can manifest an abundant life. So do what you love and turn your life into a work of art, because the world needs your imprint!

CONCLUSION

During the COVID-19 pandemic, I lost the job that I had lived and breathed for seventeen years. I had been working from home, and right before it happened, I heard, "Pray," so I did. I had no idea I was being laid off, but it was no surprise to God. He knew it was happening, and he was preparing me for it by equipping me with peace.

When it happened, I was in a nonresistant state. I was emotionally unaffected and therefore protected. I immediately went to God, saying, "I know you have a better plan for me. I know this is the beginning of something wonderful." I had been praying to God to bring my dreams to life, and now he was.

When we ask God for help, he presents us with opportunities to change. That's exactly what happened to me. I had a big decision to make: see the reality of the situation for what it was—my prayers being answered—or find another job. So, I listened to my heart and gut, which both said, *Write the book*. Then, I pulled up the anchor that was keeping me in my comfort zone, a false belief that stability is tied to the outside world. This new perspective allowed me to set sail and never look back, because I knew the truth: stability comes from within.

However, no matter how old we are or how many experiences we've had, we will be tested when we set out on a new journey. Our fears will be triggered. I wondered, *How am I going to do this? What is my future going to look like? Why do I have to go through this alone?* I had to quash these fear-based thoughts one by one.

First off: *How am I going to do this?* The key to a peaceful life is nonresistance. It's being emotionally unaffected by what is happening to you or around you. It's pushing past uncomfortable feelings and believing the outcome will be everything you desire it to be. This certainty of existence is the result of having an abundance mindset, knowing your own divinity, and putting your full trust and faith in God.

Second: *What is my future going to look like?* If you constantly worry about tomorrow, you are asleep at the wheel, using your imagination for all the wrong reasons—and attracting more challenging experiences as a result. You must anchor yourself in the now, retraining your mind to work for you. What you give conscious attention to now is what will show up in the future.

Third: *Why do I have to go through this alone?* When I had this thought, I responded, "I am not alone. God is my pilot, and I am the copilot; together, we are soaring to new heights!" How can you be alone when God resides within?

Would I have walked away from my job if I hadn't been laid off? That's a good question because my job represented stability to me, but when the opportunity presented itself to move in a new direction, I took it. I knew that I deserved more, and my desire for a new way of living outweighed the illusions that had held me back in the past.

When you have an inner knowing that it's time for a change, it's a sign that your soul is craving a new experience and wants to grow. When you do things that allow you to feel fulfilled and satisfied, you live authentically and abundantly.

Throughout this book, I've shared a few of my personal experiences to show how we continue to reaffirm false beliefs. For example, all along, I was worried about not being accepted, not knowing that I was rejecting myself because of my lack of self-worth, which didn't allow me to identify with love for self. Now that I know my worth, I no longer desire to fit in, because I know I was designed to stand out.

Life has a way of coming full circle to show us that all things work together for our greater good. How do I know? Because my life lessons, along with my rainy day fund, allowed me to write this book and help others realize their dreams.

Remember, the secret to life is to know yourself. When you know who you are and what you are capable of achieving, you won't fall for fear. Instead, you will rise in faith because you will have awakened to the truth: you are the divine designer of your destiny.

So, without further ado, *let's do this thing called life!* Let's pack a bag full of faith, belief, gratitude, passion, focus, and discipline, and take the road less traveled—the pathway to abundance. Above all, let's put God first by leading with love, so we can make our lives—and the lives of others—as extraordinary as *we* are.

In closing, I'd like to express my deepest gratitude for your valuable time and attention—thank you from the bottom of my heart. See you on the playing field of life!

—Deborah

P.S. Drop me a message when you join the 2 percent club!

Thank you in advance for scanning the QR code below to be a part of Deborah Arseneau's *Let's Do This Thing Called Life* forward-thinking community, built on a foundation of God, Christ Consciousness, and love.

ACKNOWLEDGMENTS

My heart is overflowing with gratitude as I write this thank-you note. What a wonderful feeling it is to see the seeds I've sown come to life!

I'd like to begin by thanking God for this golden opportunity that has expanded my knowledge, wisdom, and consciousness. I have learned so much from writing this book, as it has helped me grow spiritually, mentally, and emotionally. Now, I'm seeing life in a whole new light—filled with faith, hope, love, optimism, and a childlike spirit—and for that, I am eternally grateful.

It's with deep appreciation, profound thanks, and the highest respect that I acknowledge my family and friends, who are my circle of unconditional love, trust, and support. They were with me every step of the way, somehow knowing when I needed a word of encouragement, and for that, I am forever grateful and truly blessed. They are an example of what love is. I'd also like to acknowledge my loved ones in heaven and the angels who are guiding me along my new path.

I'd like to pay special homage to all the teachers in the personal development industry who've inspired me over the years and from whom I've learned so much: Bob Proctor, Neville

Goddard, Dr. Wayne Dyer, Og Mandino, Napoleon Hill, Florence Scovel Shinn, Don Miguel Ruiz, Louise Hay, and countless others.

I'd also like to express sincere thanks and appreciation to all the folks who have helped me bring this book to life. Special thanks to editors Kathleen McIntosh, Teresa K. Miller, and Nicole Jobe for making the book better; Darnah Mercieca at Books and Brand for her expertise, support, and guidance in assisting me with getting my book published and out into the world; cover designers Amy King and Lauren Smith for bringing my vision to life; Danna Mathias Steele for creating an inviting reading experience through interior design; and copywriter Skylar Griego for assistance in marketing writing.

Finally, with gratitude, I'd like to acknowledge all the souls who have crossed my path, for my life lessons have awakened me. These lessons led to my life's purpose: to be of service to others by sharing what I've learned over the years.

AUTHOR BIOGRAPHY

Deborah Arseneau began her career as a radio personality and later transitioned to media sales, where she spent most of her career. Today, she's following her lifelong passion for personal development. Deborah shares the knowledge, wisdom, and insight that she's gained along the way in the hope of helping others create their best life by living from their Higher Self—for that's where abundance lies. You can find out more about Deborah at www.deboraharseneau.com.

Let's Do This Thing Called Life!